# THE INTERNET TRAP

ASHESH MUKHERJEE

# THE INTERNET TRAP

Five Costs of Living Online

UNIVERSITY OF TORONTO PRESS
Toronto  Buffalo  London

ISBN 978-1-4426-4983-5

∞ Printed on acid-free, 100% post-consumer recycled paper
with vegetable-based inks.

_____

**Library and Archives Canada Cataloguing in Publication**

Mukherjee, Ashesh, 1968-, author
The internet trap : five costs of living online / Ashesh Mukherjee.
(Rotman-UTP Publishing)

Includes bibliographical references and index.
ISBN 978-1-4426-4983-5 (hardcover)

1. Internet – Psychological aspects.  2. Internet – Social aspects.
3. Social media – Psychological aspects.  4. Social media – Social aspects.
5. Internet addiction.  6. Social media addiction.  I. Title.

HM1017.M85 2018    302.23'1    C2017-906448-7

_____

University of Toronto Press acknowledges the financial assistance to its
publishing program of the Canada Council for the Arts and the Ontario Arts
Council, an agency of the Government of Ontario.

 **Canada Council
for the Arts**  **Conseil des Arts
du Canada**

 **ONTARIO ARTS COUNCIL
CONSEIL DES ARTS DE L'ONTARIO**
an Ontario government agency
un organisme du gouvernement de l'Ontario

Funded by the    Financé par le
Government    gouvernement
of Canada    du Canada

*To my parents, Ena and Ashim*

# CONTENTS

# PREFACE

## What Is This Book About?

We live much of our lives online. We follow friends on Facebook, browse news on the *New York Times*, share files on Dropbox, plan vacations on TripAdvisor, send messages on WhatsApp, set up dates on Match.com, shop on Amazon, watch videos on YouTube, and search for information on Google. The Internet has transformed our lives; we now have a world of information at our fingertips that we can use to make better judgments and decisions.

But is it possible that the Internet has also made life more difficult for us? Could it be that having easy access to information is a curse rather than a blessing? We will see in this book that the Internet hurts us in five important ways, which I call the five costs of living online: too much temptation, too much information, too much customization, too many comparisons, and too little privacy. Each of the five chapters describes a cost, explains its psychological origins, and suggests ways to minimize the cost. By the end of this book, you will understand why the Internet is not just a force for good but also a cause for concern. You will see how our judgments and decisions are biased when we go online, and what we can do to reduce these biases in our own lives. To take a few examples, you'll learn why:

- surfing the Internet anonymously can encourage bad behavior
- using search engines to find information can hinder our ability to learn
- using social media can make us unhappy and envious
- customizing products on the Internet can lead to overspending
- doing online research can devalue the product we finally choose

You'll also learn about techniques for avoiding these dangers and becoming a smarter user of the Internet. For example, you'll understand why:

- deciding not to choose is as important as deciding what to choose
- most of the time, we should aim for "good enough" rather than perfect choices
- we should set up structural barriers to temptations on the Internet
- we should set up systems that expose us to contrary opinions on the Internet
- we should do "cold" rather than "hot" comparisons with others on social media

## Why Did I Write This Book?

Before delving into the five costs of the Internet – what they are and what we can do about them – let me take a detour and tell you why I wrote this book, or really, why I felt compelled to write this book. My story begins in the city of Calcutta (now called Kolkata), India, where I grew up in the 1970s. This was a time before globalization and software, when India was a backwater in the world economy. There were power cuts in the evenings, and my earliest memories are doing homework by the light of a hurricane lamp. Clogged drains flooded the streets during monsoon rains, and cats, dogs, cows, people, and cars all went about their business in waist-deep water. We didn't have a television set at home, and even our neighbors who did could only watch a few black-and-white channels of propaganda from the Ministry of Information and Broadcasting. And like most people, we didn't have a telephone because there was a 20-year waiting list for a black rotary-dial phone. Don't get me wrong: life was good in ways only children appreciate, but most readers of this book have probably not experienced the economy of basic needs and primitive technology that I grew up with.

If someone had described the Internet to me when I was a child or even a teenager, it would have seemed like a science-fiction fantasy from the twenty-third century. Listening to every song ever recorded on demand? Looking up other travelers' reviews, and booking international airline tickets on my own? Video calls with friends and family on the other side of the world using a computer in my pocket? It would have seemed laughable, and certainly not on the cards during my lifetime. But as I grew older, the economy in India liberalized. Mobile phones leapfrogged rotary-dial phones, Coke and Pepsi resumed their cola wars, and the local Ambassador car was replaced by Hondas, Toyotas, and Fords. But the biggest change was the Internet. First with dial-up connections and then broadband, I saw new worlds of commerce, entertainment, dating, travel, and knowledge open up that simply did not exist before. These worlds couldn't be farther from the one I grew up in, and I could explore them simply by tapping a few keys on a computer. Given where I came from, these changes were fascinating and I never took them for granted.

At around this time, in the early 1990s, I moved to the United States to pursue a doctorate in marketing at the University of Texas at Austin. Arriving at the Austin airport on a hot August evening, I found myself at the beginning of an Internet revolution. The university had excellent network infrastructure, and the dot-com boom was about to begin. I observed how the Internet was changing the way people worked and played. I saw how it was becoming a central part of our lives, helping us keep in touch with family and friends, shop for products and services, invest money, and find communities to belong to. The conventional wisdom at the time held that the Internet was the greatest thing since sliced bread, a magic potion that would make consumers happy and companies rich. There is truth to this, and it is important to remember that the Internet has indeed brought many benefits to society.

## Benefits of the Internet

The most important benefit of the Internet is that it gives us more choices, as well as more information about these choices. Amazon offers a greater selection of books and music than any physical bookstore; Spotify offers many more stations than terrestrial radio; Netflix has more movies any physical video store; YouTube features millions of video clips; and we can buy shoes in every imaginable style on Zappos. More choices should be good for us, since having more options makes it possible to find the ideal product that's perfect for us. The Internet also offers us more information about these choices. Interested in an ecotourism trip to Bhutan? Chances are that you'll find discussions about this or any other destination you can think of on websites like TripAdvisor and Lonely Planet. As with more choices, more information about choices should be a good thing because it lets us evaluate our options in a more thorough fashion.

Information is only useful if we can find it, and it is now much easier to find information online. Search engines like Google and Bing are constantly refining their algorithms to deliver the most relevant answers to our queries, and social search engines deliver results tailored to our online profiles and those of our friends and family. Amazon and Netflix have even reduced the need to search by giving us personally relevant recommendations based on our past behavior and the choices of those similar to us. The easier it is to find relevant information online, the more useful the Internet is for making judgments and decisions.

Another advantage of the Internet is that we can analyze information to make better decisions. When we search for airline tickets on Expedia or Travelocity, we can sort the results by price, airline, travel time, or any other feature that might be important to us. Political websites ask questions about the economic, social, and political opinions of website visitors and then identify the party or candidate closest to the visitors' views. Such online tools distill insight from raw information and help us better understand our preferences for products, services, and political parties.

The Internet never sleeps; we can search and shop at our convenience, any time of the day or night. Given our busy lives, the sheer convenience of the Internet makes it an attractive platform for making choices. The Internet also permits greater customization, both for firms and for consumers. Firms can customize their offerings by tracking online behavior, analyzing search terms in Google, and pinpointing location using GPS coordinates. Similarly, consumers can tailor products to their own tastes, in categories ranging from computers to watches. The early success of Dell was based on its ability to deliver customized computers rather than the standard models offered by competitors. Swatch prospered by giving consumers the option to create custom-designed watches with unique dials, faces, and straps. The greater the ability to customize, the more likely it is that consumers will get exactly the product they are looking for, and the happier they should be with their choices.

These benefits of the Internet apply not just to product choices but also to social and recreational choices. Our social opportunities have been greatly expanded by the Internet, which offers companionship and community without the traditional constraints of place and time. We can browse thousands of prospective partners on dating websites, join Meetup groups, keep in touch on Facebook, and follow the blogs of like-minded people. Online social connections are especially important in fast-paced modern societies where close personal ties are often difficult to forge. And the Internet offers new ways to cultivate our interests and expand our horizons. Regardless of whether we're in Toronto or Timbuktu, we can learn at our own pace by following online courses, video clips, and discussion boards about issues close to our hearts.

## Costs of the Internet

Although there are many benefits of the Internet, I found myself wondering if the Internet – or technology in general – also has a dark side. I got an opportunity to explore this issue when I was thinking about my dissertation research. The dissertation is the culmination of a doctoral program, where a PhD student focuses on a research question and conducts a scientific investigation to answer this question. One of the pleasures of academia is that researchers can investigate any issue that interests them personally, so I decided to pursue why people respond differently to technological products. For readers younger than a certain age, technology is second or even first nature. When I teach at university, my students usually have one eye on me – if I'm lucky – and their other eye fixed firmly on a phone, tablet, or laptop, and sometimes all three at once. Our daughter learned to swipe and select cartoons on the iPad by herself when she was less than a year old. Other people, however, have a more adversarial relationship with technology. If you think about your grandparents, parents, or older relatives, you probably know a few people who are allergic to high-technology products. My mother, for instance, firmly believes that the iPad she was given is her sworn enemy, with a ghost in the machine who takes personal pleasure in sabotaging her FaceTime sessions.

Given the prevalence of technophobia in modern society, I thought it would be interesting to study this phenomenon in my doctoral dissertation. To my surprise, I found that although technophobia was a term in common usage, it was defined rather loosely and there was little scientific research into its psychological causes. My own intuition suggested that learning cost – i.e., time and effort required to learn new technologies – might be an important reason for technophobia. Other researchers had already shown that negative information has a bigger effect on our opinions than positive information, so I thought negative learning costs should have a bigger effect on people's attitudes towards technological products than the positive benefits likely to be delivered by these products. I tested these ideas in a series of research studies where I showed different groups of people various high-tech products, such as new computers and phones, and measured their responses, such as their attitudes towards these products, expected learning costs, and expected benefits. I found that, as predicted, perceived learning costs often overshadow the future benefits of high-tech products, especially when the complexity of the product is high. Thus, learning costs are an important driver of technophobia.

After completing my doctorate, I started working as a professor in the business school at McGill University in Montreal. During my research career, I have conducted many studies on the effects of the Internet and other technologies on consumers. A general finding in my research was that the Internet has significant costs that are often overlooked by its users. For example, I found that information overload on the Internet can lead to poorer decision-making, and social comparisons on social media can undermine our happiness and well-being. I also found that other researchers were reporting similar results, namely that the Internet imposes costs on users that are not always easy to anticipate in advance.

The more I learned, the more I saw the need to bring this growing body of research to an audience beyond academia. So I decided to write a book that would summarize key research findings about the costs of the Internet, in simple language accessible to general readers. Equally important, I wanted to examine some fundamental questions about the nature of modern life. Thanks to mobile devices like smartphones, tablets, and wearable technology, the Internet has become our constant companion. Before long, we will live in a world where the Internet of things, and perhaps biologically implanted Internet, will become commonplace. The line between online and offline will become blurred and, like the movie *Matrix*, the network will be everywhere. Do we understand the implications of this brave new world? What can we do to benefit from the upsides and avoid the downsides of the Internet? These are the questions I want to explore in this book.

## What Does This Book Cover?

This book describes five costs of the Internet – five ways in which the Internet biases our judgments and decisions, reflected in the chapter titles: "Too Many Temptations," "Too Much Information," "Too Much Customization," "Too Many Comparisons," and "Too Little Privacy." Chapter 1 shows that the Internet reduces our self-control and makes it easy to overindulge. Chapter 2 points out that having a world of information at our fingertips can paradoxically make it more difficult to make good choices. Chapter 3 discusses why having it our way can set us up for disappointment. Chapter 4 shows that we often compare ourselves with others on the Internet in ways that make us less happy and productive. Chapter 5 reveals that people say they have little privacy on the Internet but then behave online as if no one is watching. The conclusion summarizes the central themes of the book and looks into the future of our relationship with the Internet.

The five costs discussed in this book can be grouped into two categories: commercial costs for consumers, and social costs for individuals. The costs in the first two chapters – too many temptations and too much information – are relevant to consumers, while the costs in the next three chapters – too much customization, too many comparisons, and too little privacy – apply to both consumers and individuals. To be clear, this book is not intended as a comprehensive listing of all the costs of the Internet. Besides the five costs described in this book, the Internet could be harmful for us in other ways as well. For example, spending more time on the Internet could reduce face-to-face interaction, leading to greater social isolation and reduced social skills. Constantly switching between phones, tablets, laptops, and wearables could reduce our attention span and ability to focus on extended tasks. Citizens who become dependent on the Internet for information could be manipulated by governments that control information or plant fake news online. I have chosen to focus on five important costs in this book that I have personal knowledge of, through either my own research or the research of my academic colleagues. I believe this approach makes the book more reliable by basing its conclusions on scientific evidence.

There are two other features of this book worth mentioning. First, each chapter explains the psychological reasons underlying the costs of living online. For example, the effect of too much information on the Internet is explained using psychological concepts such as the limited information processing capacity of our minds and our use of mental shortcuts to simplify choices. Similarly, other costs are explained using psychological concepts like self-control, confirmation bias, social norms, hedonic treadmill, and reference point. Understanding the psychological underpinnings of the five costs will help the reader understand where these costs are coming from. And second, each chapter ends with solutions – actionable steps that we can take to minimize the five costs and thus maximize the benefits of the Internet in our own lives.

## How Does Research Inform This Book?

As mentioned earlier, this book is based on scientific research and not on conjecture or personal anecdotes. Many researchers, including myself, have conducted studies on the effects of the Internet. These studies, however, have mostly been published in specialized journals aimed at an academic audience and written in technical language not always intelligible to lay readers. Research findings are also scattered across different journals, making it difficult to see the forest for the trees. This book is useful because it condenses a large body of academic research into five key costs of the Internet and describes these costs in simple language illustrated with everyday examples.

A broader objective of this book is to foster greater understanding of the scientific method as a key for unlocking the secrets of our world. When we think of scientists, we usually imagine white-coated chemists or biologists studying the natural world in laboratories or in the field. What is perhaps less well known is that social scientists use similar methods to understand the social world, consisting of people and their interactions with technology. What is the scientific method? To simplify, the scientific method consists of asking questions about the world and collecting data to answer these questions. Data can sometimes be qualitative, as with interviews, focus groups, and ethnographic observations. At other times, data can be quantitative, such as responses to surveys, behavior in experimental laboratories, and actual behavior in daily life.

Although both qualitative and quantitative data are useful to answer questions in the social sciences, this book focuses on quantitative data based on experiments. The goal of an experiment is to understand cause and effect: for example, the causes of technophobia, spending during Christmas holidays, or customer satisfaction for products and services. Experiments pinpoint cause and effect by isolating a particular cause and slowing down the underlying psychological process so we can observe how the cause influences the effect. Reading a description of an experiment is a bit like watching a movie in slow motion – we can see events unfold in detail and thus see exactly how the cause leads to the effect. I focus on experimental research in this book for a simple reason – my training is in experimental social science, and I have personally conducted many experiments to study the psychology of the Internet. I am also well informed about experimental research conducted by others through my participation in academic conferences and work as a reviewer for academic journals. Since experiments are an important research tool, I would like readers to gain a better understanding of how experiments are conducted in the social sciences. To this end, I will describe many interesting experiments throughout the book, often with insider details not reported in the published articles. I have written these descriptions with a general audience in mind, to convey essential aspects of the experiments without burdening the reader with unnecessary minutiae.

## How Should You Read This Book?

I suggest reading the chapters in the order in which they appear. Psychological concepts introduced in earlier chapters are sometimes used again later with the assumption that readers are familiar with them. The five costs are also organized in a sequence from consumer-related to individual-related. This book will be most useful if readers can see the relevance of the five costs to their own lives. To help make these personal connections, the book includes many real-world examples and case studies. Readers will further benefit by thinking about how the five costs apply to their own experiences with the Internet. The more actively and critically you consider the ideas in this book, the more you will understand and perhaps challenge the conclusions of this book. If you feel informed and stimulated after reading this book, I will consider my writing to be successful.

To sum up, here's how you can benefit from this book – whether you are a curious person interested in the Internet or a manager interested in the business implications of the Internet. The Internet has become an essential part of our lives and represents a significant change in our physical and social environment. During thousands of years of human evolution, information search consisted of seeking out personally known experts rather than doing a Google search. Choice consisted of picking from a limited number of products at local markets rather than unlimited choices from around the world. Social networks did not mean hundreds of Facebook friends or Twitter followers but the few people we actually met and interacted with face-to-face on a daily basis. Education was for the elite, based on books and manuscripts locked inside schools, bookstores, libraries, or monasteries. Our minds were shaped in this simpler environment, which has been upended in the evolutionary blink of an eye. After reading this book, you will better understand the implications of this fundamental shift in our environment – what are its dangers and what steps we can take to avoid these dangers. You will also gain broader insights into human psychology – how people think and act – and be able to use these insights to make better decisions in your own life.

I believe ideas improve through dialogue and feedback. If you have any comments, suggestions, or criticisms about this book, I would love to hear from you at ashesh.mukherjee@mcgill.ca. Let's get started.

Ashesh Mukherjee
Montreal, Canada

# THE INTERNET TRAP

# TOO MANY TEMPTATIONS

When was the last time you starting browsing the Web for "only a few minutes" but ended up spending more than an hour on your favorite websites? Have you ever visited an online store "just to look" but left with a lighter wallet? Have you looked at a deal on Amazon or Groupon and impulsively clicked the "buy now" button? If you said yes or even maybe to any of these questions, you've heard the call of temptation on the Internet. In addition to our hard-earned money, we spend much of our limited time on social media, games, blogs, videos, music, news, and online chat. Add it up and we can see that temptations for spending time and money are multiplying on the Internet. And these temptations will only increase in the future as the Internet offers ever more brands, retailers, entertainment, and media from around the world.

## The Costs of Temptation

Temptations present us with a dilemma: Should we resist in the interest of long-term goals such as saving money for retirement, or should we indulge for the sake of immediate pleasure? Giving in to temptation is not always a bad thing. We sometimes find great deals online for spas, restaurants, and vacations – things that make life more fun at a price within our reach. We sometimes expand our horizons by stumbling across new music, movies, books, and points of view that we might never have considered otherwise. At other times, however, temptation has a cost. Online sales events can tempt us into buying things we neither need nor can afford. Buying a new handbag, smartphone, or watch might make us feel good momentarily, but the credit card bill later will bring us back to earth. The most depressing day of the year is said to be "blue Monday" – a Monday in the middle in the January – when the glow of Christmas has worn off, summer vacations are far away, and the credit card bills start arriving. The more we spend today, the more debt we incur, the less savings we have, and the less is our security in old age. Wasting time is also costly; the more time we spend online, the less time we have for our loved ones and the less productive we are at work.

Giving in to temptation not only has short-term costs – credit card bills and missed deadlines – but also long-term implications for success and happiness in life. Researchers at Stanford University examined this issue in a study conducted in the 1960s which has become famous as the "marshmallow experiment" (Mischel, Ebbesen, & Raskoff Zeiss, 1972). These researchers wanted to answer a simple question: Do children with more self-control enjoy greater success and happiness in adult life, compared to children with lower self-control? The researchers suspected that the answer was yes, because children who show higher self-control are likely to have desirable personality traits such as focus and perseverance that favor greater success in adult life as well.

So what might tempt a child? Obviously candies and snacks, which the researchers used as temptations in this study. The researchers went to a nursery school near San Francisco and secured permission to recruit children between the ages of four and six to take part in the study. The children were brought one by one into an empty room and seated at a table facing a bowl of their favorite treat. This was a bowl of marshmallows – hence the name of the experiment – but other treats such as Oreo cookies and pretzel sticks were also used in later studies. The children were told that the teacher would leave the room for 15 minutes, and while waiting for their teacher to come back, they could have one (and only one) marshmallow if they wanted. If, however, they waited for the teacher to come back without eating anything, they could have two marshmallows instead of one. The teacher then left the room and the children's behavior was secretly recorded for the next 15 minutes.

What did the researchers find? Their first finding is not particularly surprising, especially for those of us who have children. Of the 600 or so children who participated in the experiment, more than 60 percent did not wait for 15 minutes to collect their two promised marshmallows, instead promptly eating one marshmallow in their teacher's absence. The researchers then observed these two groups of children – those who ate one marshmallow without waiting, and those who waited for their two marshmallows – for the next 30 years. What they found was quite remarkable. The children who gave in to temptation during the experiment by eating a marshmallow as soon as the teacher left did worse than those who waited on many indicators of success, such as school grades, SAT scores, income, divorce rates, and physical health. On all of these outcomes, the conclusion was clear – the ability to resist temptation and postpone gratification at an early age, on a seemingly minor task, was related to many later successes in life.

Of course, there is an important caveat for studies like this which unfold over an extended period of time. It is possible that the two groups of children in the study – those who waited and those who did not – had different life experiences after the marshmallow task, and these life experiences could be driving the difference in outcomes between the groups. Even allowing for this caveat, it is worth noting that the results were consistent across virtually every measure in the study, suggesting that its basic finding is reliable – early self-control in the face of temptation is an indicator of later success in life.

Another danger is that temptations can sometimes mutate into addiction. An addiction is where a person engages in activity that is pleasurable at the present moment but harmful to other responsibilities in life such as work, relationships, or health. Three types of addictive behaviors are especially prevalent on the Internet: gaming, shopping, and pornography. Gaming has grown from simple Pac-Man-style arcade entertainment to complex online games such as World of Warcraft, featuring multiple levels, intricate plots, and multiplayer interaction. Addiction to online gaming seems to be greater among teenagers in South Korea, China, and the United States (Ferguson, 2010). Hardcore gamers are known to spend more than 18 hours a day playing online games, in a thriving gamer subculture with its own discussion boards, tournaments, and annual conventions. Online shopping is another form of addiction, and some have estimated that 5–8 percent of Americans compulsively buy things online (Trotzke, Starcke, Müller, & Brand, 2015). Pornography is yet another popular pastime on the Internet. Depending on the survey, between 25 percent and 40 percent of men – but far fewer women – say they watch online pornography on a regular basis, and more than half of all online search words are related to pornography (Griffiths, 2001). Even if a small percentage of those who watch online pornography are addicted, it would still constitute a significant number of Internet users.

We have seen that the Internet tempts us in many ways, and giving in to temptation has significant costs in the form of reduced chances of success in life, diminished happiness, and increased risk of addiction. But is the Internet uniquely tempting? Temptations have been with us forever, starting with the apple in the Garden of Eden and in modern times with books, movies, supermarkets, malls, television, video games, and now the Internet. We will see that the Internet is an especially seductive incarnation of temptation because it undermines us in two important ways at the same time – it increases our desires and lowers our self-control.

## Increased Desire

Desire is the wish for something – the stronger the wish, the greater is desire. The intensity of desire is said to depend on the gap between our ideal and actual states (Baumeister, 2002). Let's illustrate this with an example. Imagine you're browsing an Ikea store for home decor ideas. The actual state here would be your own home with all its flaws and charms – worn furniture, missing cutlery, dated lighting, and unkempt garden. The ideal state would be the staged home display in Ikea showing its latest products, furnishings, and accessories. As you've probably noticed, the staged displays at Ikea are designed to look like perfect homes that we can easily compare in our mind's eye with our not-so-perfect homes. It is this gap between actual and ideal states that creates desire and tempts us into buying things. Of course, there are many other aspects of stores like Ikea that encourage impulsive shopping – like putting attractive items at the entrance and giving extra-large shopping bags to customers – but let's focus for the moment on actual and ideal states. The Internet has magnified the gap between ideal and actual states and thereby strengthened our desire to spend money and time online.

### Ideal States

Imagine you're looking for a hotel to stay in during your upcoming vacation. If you search on TripAdvisor or Hotels.com, you can see the best hotels of the world with professionally shot pictures, videos, and even 3D walkthroughs of their stunning premises. Instagram is full of perfect pictures of jewelry, meals, beaches, clothes, and concerts. Reddit has pages devoted to food porn, where users post perfect pictures of meals in exotic settings. If you search for watches, electronics, or shoes online, you will find websites filled with desirable brands from around the world. If you are looking for love, you can browse dozens of dating websites featuring more attractive members than you could ever possibly meet in the real world.

The Internet is full of desirable options, options which are really a barrage of ideal states that follow us wherever we go. People now surf the Internet anytime anywhere using smartphones and tablets, and this constant immersion in the online world has increased our exposure to ideal states. The more we see ideal states, the greater is the gap between these ideals and our actual states, and the stronger is our desire to reduce this gap by purchasing products and services. Social media plays an important part in this process. When I first started using Facebook, I was curious about my friends and family and regularly browsed their status updates and pictures. I soon got the feeling that everyone except me was having a good time: partying, traveling, dining, and shopping. Could it be that that my friends have exceptionally interesting lives? Was my life really so boring in comparison? Or is it possible that people are posting only their happy stuff on Facebook? To answer these questions, I conducted a research study where I asked students at my university to look at pictures posted by their Facebook friends and to classify these pictures into three categories: those that showed people having a good time versus a neutral time versus a bad time (Auschaitrakul & Mukherjee, 2014). The results couldn't be clearer. The vast majority of pictures posted on Facebook were of people having a good time, with some neutral pictures thrown in and hardly any negative pictures. If we went by Facebook postings, we would conclude that life is a whirl of parties, beach vacations, and trips to Vegas. But common sense and personal experience tell us that life is not always perfect, and people are probably cherry-picking their best experiences to post on social media. Social media is putting a filter on our view of the world, showing a collage of ideal states that hides the more humdrum reality of our lives. Constant exposure to these ideal states will increase the gap between our actual lives and the idealized lives we see online, leading to greater desire for things we don't have.

Another way the Internet increases desire is by tailoring ideal states to our unique needs and wants. If you type a term into a Google search, the ads that appear will be based on your search term, browsing history, and Gmail profile. If you log in to websites using your Facebook account, you will soon start receiving online offers tailored to your Facebook profile, likes and dislikes on Facebook, and Facebook friends' likes and dislikes. Stores often send text messages with coupons to mobile phone users who are physically close to the store, and customers within stores receive offers specific to the aisle they are browsing in. These tailored offers constitute ideal states engineered to be highly relevant to our specific needs and wants at that particular time. Because we pay more attention to personally relevant information (Pieters & Warlop, 1999), tailored ideal states stand out and contrast more sharply with actual states in our minds. This heightened contrast increases the intensity of desire and the likelihood of us giving in to temptation.

Ideal states are often presented on websites in an audiovisual format with pictures, video, and sound. Evolutionary psychology suggests that audiovisual information is likely to have a bigger effect on our judgments and decisions than written information (Confer, Perilloux, & Buss, 2010). For millennia, our hunter-gatherer ancestors relied on their eyes and ears – not written instructions – to hunt for food, avoid predators, and find mates. Because of this history, our brains have evolved to rely primarily on audiovisual information. So when we see videos or pictures online, we are engaging a part of the brain that has evolved to process information quickly and generate strong emotions. If you look at online games like World of Warcraft or Halo, you will see that they effectively use audiovisual design to hook users. These games feature immersive environments that mimic the sights and sounds our brains have been trained to respond to over thousands of years and so provide a primeval pleasure that makes gamers susceptible to addiction. Virtual reality headsets will soon make immersive experiences commonplace, and we will be living in realistic virtual worlds full of ideal states. Imagine going on a virtual reality tour of Bora Bora or Ibiza and then setting out on your daily commute through smog and traffic. Wouldn't you be tempted to book your next vacation right away?

## Actual States

Another way the Internet increases desire is by reminding us of our low actual states. Before the Internet, we were often unaware of our actual states on a moment-to-moment basis. We received snail mail once a day and bank statements once a month. In contrast, we can now check our investments, emails, and text messages whenever we want. These up-to-the-second updates make our actual states visible to us at all times. And the more we are aware of our actual states, the easier it is to compare actual and ideal states and to experience stronger feelings of desire.

Unfortunately, our minds are wired to keep ideal states above actual states through a psychological process called the hedonic treadmill (Loewenstein, 2005). The hedonic treadmill is a tendency for people to automatically move their ideal states upward over time, thus creating a permanent gap between ideal and actual states. For example, if we own an iPhone, the hedonic treadmill makes us want the latest model – the ideal state – even if the model we currently own works just fine. Research suggests that the hedonic treadmill might run faster when we are exposed to new ideal states on a regular basis (Diener, Lucas, & Scollon, 2006). This is bad news for us, because seeing a constant stream of new products online will quickly move our ideal states upward to the next object of desire. The hedonic treadmill also explains the attraction of Internet pornography – the more often we see arousing images online, the more likely we are to raise our ideal states for gratification. In this way, the gap between ideal and actual is maintained, leading to an endless and ultimately futile quest for pleasure.

## Lower Self-Control

The Internet makes us vulnerable to temptation by reducing self-control. Self-control is our mental capacity to make choices that favor long-term over short-term goals (Ainslie, 1992; Faber & Vohs, 2004). We often have long-term goals that are accomplished over an extended period of time, such as being healthy, staying fit, losing weight, saving money, getting a promotion, or learning a new language. In addition, we also have short-term goals pursued in the here and now, such as completing a school assignment, closing a sale, or savoring a fine Scotch whisky. Remember the marshmallow experiment? The children who chose to eat one marshmallow right away showed lower self-control because they focused on the short-term goal of instant pleasure rather than the long-term goal of maximizing marshmallows. We shall see that our self-control is often lower when we go online because of goal conflict, goal clarity, the foot-in-the-door effect, lower energy, and product pricing on the Internet.

### Goal Conflict

Imagine it's a Friday evening. Your friends are planning to meet for dinner and then go partying at the new club downtown. You feel torn because, although you would love to join them, you have a big exam coming up on Monday that you need to study for. This is an example of goal conflict: two goals – partying and studying – are pulling you in different directions. Research suggests that failing to resolve goal conflict early weakens our self-control, making it more likely that we will ultimately give in to temptation (Stroebe, Mensink, Aarts, Schut, & Kruglanski, 2008). For example, if we are facing a goal conflict between partying and studying, we are more likely to end up partying if we put off resolving this conflict until the last minute. In contrast, if we resolve this conflict early by thinking about the pros and cons of studying versus partying, we are more likely to stay in and study for the exam.

Goal conflict often arises online as well. When we idly browse Amazon or eBay "just to look," we have probably not clarified in our own mind whether we are looking for a cheaper product or a higher-quality product. Price and quality are conflicting goals, since it is difficult if not impossible to pay the lowest price and get the highest-quality product. Failing to decide in advance whether price or quality is more important creates goal conflict. This goal conflict reduces self-control, making it more likely that we will end up buy something impulsively online.

## Goal Clarity

Another factor that reduces self-control is lack of goal clarity (Campbell et al., 1996). This is why window shoppers usually make more impulse purchases than those with a shopping list in hand. The act of writing a shopping list clarifies our shopping goals by expressing clearly what we are looking for. Those without a shopping list, in contrast, have not clarified their shopping goals, which undermines their self-control when they are faced with temptation. The Internet has made it easier for us to window-shop because we can now effortlessly browse many websites without getting up from the couch. The more we browse in this manner without clear shopping goals, the lower will be our self-control and the higher will be the likelihood of buying something on impulse.

## Foot-in-the-Door

Browsing products on the Internet can reduce our self-control because of the foot-in-the-door effect (Cialdini, 2001). Foot-in-the-door is a psychological process whereby taking a small step towards an object increases the chances that we will take a bigger step towards the same object later. Car salespeople sometimes use foot-in-the-door to influence customers. Imagine you're at a dealership checking out your favorite car. As you're admiring the vehicle, a salesperson approaches and offers you an attractive price – lower than you had expected to pay – on the condition that you complete the paperwork right away. You accept the offer since the price is great and you wanted this car anyway. The salesperson then takes your completed forms to the manager's office for final approval. Minutes turn into an hour while you cool your heels at the salesperson's desk. At last, the salesperson emerges and says apologetically that he did his best but his manager simply would not approve the price offered earlier. Instead, the salesperson now offers you a higher "final price" that is supposedly the absolute best price he could get you. In situations like this, many customers agree to buy at the higher "final price" even if this price was more than what the customer had originally intended to pay. This is an example of foot-in-the-door because filling out the paperwork is a small step towards the car, which increases the chances of the later (and bigger) step of actually buying the car. Similarly, browsing the websites of online retailers is a small step towards the products being offered, which is a foot-in-the-door towards our eventual purchase of these products.

## Lower Energy

Research shows that self-control depends on our energy level: the more tired we are mentally or physically, the less self-control we have (Muraven & Baumeister, 2000). For example, studies have shown that asking people to resist the urge to eat chocolate cookies placed in front of them makes them less persistent when solving math problems later. Resisting the urge to eat cookies tires us out mentally, which reduces the self-control we need to solve math problems. Similarly, the more time we spend walking around a mall – and hence the more physically tired we get – the more likely we are to buy things on impulse (Baumeister, 2002).

When we browse on eBay or Amazon, we are constantly resisting temptation in the form of attractive products and services. The resulting mental effort can tire us out and eventually reduce our self-control. The process of ordering products online also reduces our self-control. Unlike buying pizza at a food court, where we usually make up our minds quickly, ordering pizza online from Domino's or Pizza Hut is a more leisurely affair. We can take our time to browse the extensive selection of crusts, toppings, and desserts, every option being illustrated with professionally shot, mouth-watering pictures. The more we browse under these circumstances, the less our self-control and the bigger our waistlines. And when we are ready to order online, we are often asked if we want to "cheese it up" or upsize the drink for a few cents. If we have already spent $15 on a pizza, what's a few cents more for extra toppings or a larger drink?

If self-control requires mental energy, an important corollary is that we need time to summon our mental energy when we are ready to make a choice. Online services like Snapchat feature short-lived "disappearing" messages that reduce the time available to think through our responses and thus reduce our self-control. The idea that tiredness reduces self-control also applies to the marshmallow experiment discussed earlier. Recall that children in the marshmallow experiment were asked to resist temptation in the form of forbidden sweets staring them in the face. If resisting temptation makes us tired, then the children who successfully waited for 15 minutes without eating any marshmallows probably had lower self-control immediately after the experiment. As time went by, however, their energy levels – and hence self-control – went back up, along with the increased self-confidence that comes from having proved their capacity for self-control. Confidence in one's ability to exert self-control would then create a virtuous cycle of greater self-control that shows up as better choices over a lifetime.

## Product Pricing

Another way the Internet reduces self-control is through all-inclusive product pricing, such as unlimited movies on Netflix, songs on Spotify, or TV shows on Hulu for a flat monthly fee. Research indicates that people often overestimate how much they will use a product after buying it (Goodman & Irmak, 2013). Thus, if we sign up for Netflix, we are likely to imagine that we will watch a lot of movies every month because, well, we've already paid for it. In fact, most people end up watching fewer movies on Netflix than they expected to. This overestimation bias for future consumption is even stronger when the product is available in large quantities. The virtually unlimited selection of music on Spotify might lead us to believe that we will listen to a large number of songs every month to take full advantage of the service. The more we overestimate our future usage, the more likely we are to subscribe to online services offering all-inclusive pricing.

The Internet reduces our self-control in other ways as well. Research has found that people are loath to give up something they already have, since losses loom larger in our minds than gains (Tversky & Kahneman, 1983). This is why many of us hang on to our cable TV subscriptions with more than 100 channels – most of which we never watch – because the psychological pain of giving up channels outweighs the gain from paying less on our cable bill. Another aspect of the Internet that reduces self-control is the "buy now" or "one-click purchase" buttons often seen on e-commerce websites such as Amazon and iTunes. These buttons shorten the time between consideration of a product and its purchase, thus reducing our ability to muster the mental energy needed for self-control (Loewenstein, 1996).

The Internet can create a state of "flow" where we lose track of time (Csikszentmihalyi, 1996). Flow happens when we are doing highly interesting tasks that are moderately challenging. Online games often induce a state of flow, because they are designed to be very engaging and reasonably challenging at each level of game play. Online games are also designed to remain interesting after repeated use because players are always being moved into higher levels of game play with new plot elements. A state of flow while playing online games makes it difficult to keep track of time and thus increases time wasted online.

Research shows that frequent Facebook users buy more products and services than occasional users of social media (Wilcox & Stephen, 2013). Thus, the increasing use of social media around the world might lead to more online shopping, especially when more online retailers start offering one-click purchase of products mentioned in social conversations. Facebook advertising also increases online purchases because this form of advertising is tailored to our unique preferences as expressed in our Facebook profile, likes and dislikes, and recent browsing history. And finally, failures of self-control can create a vicious cycle of negative emotions and lower self-control (Atalay & Meloy, 2011). When we succumb to temptation and buy something we know we shouldn't have, we often feel guilty and ashamed. To counteract these negative emotions, we might undertake shopping therapy to feel better about ourselves. But these new purchases only end up making us feel worse, fueling a downward spiral of negative emotions and overindulgence.

## What Can We Do?

We have seen that temptations on the Internet can lead us astray. The good news is that we can take several steps to keep this danger at bay: set up structural barriers to temptation, pre-commit to pleasure, increase goal clarity, visualize positive outcomes, revoke the license to sin, create positive habits, and increase belief in our self-control.

### Structural Barriers

A useful technique for increasing self-control is to set up structural barriers to temptation (Ajzen, 2002). We can think of structural barriers as moats that we dig in our "cold" or rational moments between ourselves and objects of desire, barriers that can't be easily crossed in "hot" or tempting moments. This is not a new idea. In Homer's *Odyssey*, Ulysses asked his sailors to tie him to a mast before their ship approached the island of Sirens. This was a wise precaution; Ulysses knew that hearing the Sirens' sweet melody would render him incapable of rational thought, and he would jump to his death trying to reach the island of pleasure.

Similar to Ulysses, problem gamblers can put themselves on exclusion lists from casinos before the gambling bug bites; drivers can install car breathalyzers in their sober moments; and smokers can choose to live far from smoky bars. In all these cases, people are setting up external restraints on their behavior before temptation strikes. Other examples of structural barriers are hiding friends on Facebook to avoid seeing their postings or deleting the Facebook application itself from smartphones. To minimize wasting time on the Internet, we can install software that limits the number of websites we can access and the amount of time we can spend online in any given day. We could also install software designed to block pornographic, gambling, or gaming websites. An important characteristic of successful structural barriers is that they must be difficult to reverse in our "hot" moments. This principle is baked into commercial software for restricting Internet use, since they require users to jump through many hoops before their settings can be changed. Going through an extended modification process gives users the opportunity to think about what they are doing, thus increasing their self-control in the face of temptation.

## Pre-commitment to Pleasure

Another technique for increasing self-control is pre-commitment to pleasure. For example, we might recognize that quitting Facebook completely is unrealistic. So instead of deleting Facebook from our devices, we might set aside a designated block of time every day for browsing Facebook. If we're addicted to online shopping, we could set aside a budget at the beginning of each month for online purchases. Setting budgets is also useful because it allows us to track our behavior against the budget. We can now do this easily with apps that track how much money we spend, how many steps we have walked, and how many calories we have burned every day. Data about our behavior can be accumulated over time and compared to our targets for saving or exercise. If we see that our behavior is meeting or exceeding targets, we are likely to have greater self-control going forward. If, on the other hand, our behavior falls short of targets, we could consider setting lower targets because meeting more achievable targets is likely to increase our self-control in the future.

## Goal Clarity

Since self-control increases with goal clarity, we should make an effort to clarify our goals before browsing e-commerce retailers. For example, we could decide in advance to look only at a limited number of brands before we purchase and decide early on which features are more or less important to us. We can increase our self-control by going online earlier in the day when we have more energy, rather than later in the day when we have less energy after hours of working and commuting.

## Visualize Positive Outcomes

We can increase our self-control by visualizing positive outcomes. For example, if we want to save money, we could put pictures of our dream retirement home as the screen saver on our computers, tablets, and smartphones. This would remind us of the goal we are working towards, thus increasing our motivation to pursue this goal. In the abstract, most of us know that our savings earns compound interest to grow exponentially over time. But many people miss out on the magic of compounding by finding excuses to delay long-term savings in favor of more tempting immediate pleasures. To make the benefits of compounding come alive, we could set up a spreadsheet on our mobile device that displays the future compounded value of our monthly savings plan if we save on a daily basis. This compounded future value is likely to be a large number, which will increase our motivation for saving every day.

## License to Sin

We should be careful about acting impulsively after we have done good deeds: research shows that we feel licensed to sin as a reward for good behavior (Khan, Dhar, & Wertenbroch, 2005). For example, if we have just completed an assignment or recently given to a charity, we should be extra careful about our shopping behavior thereafter. If we do buy things, we should prefer to buy experiences such as travel and dance lessons, rather than physical products such as watches or phones, because research shows that consuming experiences usually makes us happier in the long run than accumulating physical products (Van Boven & Gilovich, 2003).

## New Habits

Temptations can harden into habit over time. If someone feels they can't stop looking at online pornography, it could be because pornography has become an automatic response to external and internal cues. For example, sitting down at the computer when no one is around can be an external cue triggering the habitual behavior of browsing pornographic websites. Similarly, feelings of boredom or stress could serve as internal triggers for pornography. An important characteristic of strong habits is that they are difficult to change head-on. Habits once learned create grooves in the mind that rarely disappear completely. Instead, a more effective approach is to create parallel grooves – parallel good habits that replace bad habits over time (Wood & Neal, 2007). For example, if sitting down at the computer is associated with pornography or wasting time online, we can start a new habit of checking our email first when we go online. And while doing so, we could send an email to ourselves listing the things we need to accomplish today. If repeated regularly, this good habit will gradually supplant our bad habits and increase our daily productivity.

## Belief in Self-Control

It is important to believe that we have a large mental store of self-control that we can draw upon whenever needed. This was shown in a research study that looked at people's New Year resolutions (Mukhopadhyay & Johar, 2005). Participants in this study were recruited in November, when most people are starting to think about resolutions for the next year. One group of participants was asked to read scientific articles stating that self-control is a limited mental resource that can easily be exhausted, while another group read articles stating that self-control is an unlimited resource that can be drawn upon whenever needed. The two groups were then asked to write down their New Year resolutions for the next year. In February, respondents were contacted again and asked to report the extent to which they had kept their resolutions. Results showed that belief about self-control matters for both setting and keeping resolutions. Those who believed self-control was an unlimited resource that can be drawn upon whenever needed set more New Year resolutions than those who thought self-control was a limited resource. And those who set more resolutions also tended to follow through and accomplish more of their goals over time. The moral of this study is that it is important to believe our self-control has no upper limit, because thinking optimistically about our capacity for self-control makes us stronger in the face of temptation.

# 2

# TOO MUCH INFORMATION

The next time you visit your local supermarket, look around at the sheer variety of products on offer. Britain's Tesco carries 91 different shampoos, 93 types of toothpaste, and 115 household cleaners (The Tyranny of Choice, 2010). The average American supermarket carries almost 50,000 items, more than five times the number available in 1975. If you think this is a lot of choice, consider the Internet, which features products from all the world's supermarkets, bookstores, electronic stores, clothing stores, and movie theatres. Not just products themselves – we now have access to more information about these products than ever before. If you are interested in a car, you can go online to learn about features, user reviews, reliability records, ownership cost, retail prices, service quality, and recall history. If you want to see a movie, you can read hundreds of reviews on Rotten Tomatoes and browse thousands of titles on Netflix. If you're looking for love, you can join dating websites for every taste and persuasion, with millions of new members signing up all the time. The Internet has vastly expanded our horizons, from a world of limited choices bounded by our physical location to a world of virtually infinite choices. But does all this information about choices really benefit us?

From a broad economic perspective, it could be argued that giving people more information is a good thing. Choice is the basis of free markets, driving competition and economic growth. At a personal level as well, choice gives us the power to pick products and services that best fit our needs. The process of choosing helps us understand our preferences and satisfies our need for variety. Choice gives us a sense of control, which is fundamental to our well-being as individuals. And from a social point of view, choices help us signal our identity and broadcast our status to others. The clothes we wear, the brand of beer we drink, and the car we drive tell others whether we are bankers, plumbers, artists, students, or hipsters; how much we earn; and what we value in life. All these benefits of choice are important. But if we look more deeply, we can see hidden dangers in a world of too much information. In fact, research has shown that too much information is bad for us in four important ways: choice paralysis, choice shortcuts, post-choice dissatisfaction, and barriers to learning.

## Choice Paralysis

Imagine you're in the ice cream aisle of your local supermarket. As you peer into the freezers, you see different flavors, brands, and packages – chocolate, caramel, praline, strawberry, mango, lychee, and coffee; gelato, sorbet, and frozen yogurt; soya and milk; Häagen-Dazs, Nestlé, and Ben & Jerry's; tubs, sticks, cones, and cookies. How do all these options affect our decision to buy ice cream? A research study looked at this situation and found that having too many choices can paralyze people into postponing their decisions (Iyengar, 2011). Researchers in this study set up a booth in a California gourmet market with a display of Wilkin & Sons jams. Every couple of hours, they changed the display from a large selection of 24 jams to a smaller selection of 6 jams. The researchers then tracked the percentage of market visitors who stopped at the booth and the percentage who bought jams there. They found that a larger assortment of jams attracted more customers to the booth, with 60 percent of visitors stopping to look at the larger selection but only 40 percent stopping at the smaller selection. More interestingly, they found that only 3 percent of people who stopped to look at the larger selection of jams actually bought something, whereas almost 30 percent of customers who stopped at the smaller selection bought at least one jar of jam. Similar studies with wine, chocolate, and retirement plans have reached the same conclusion: offering too many options can lead to choice paralysis whereby many people walk away without picking anything. And even when they do buy, people faced with excess choice spend an inordinate amount of time making up their minds. These findings have important implications for consumers and firms. If consumers are paralyzed by too much choice, they will waste valuable time on the choice process – time that could have been better spent on more productive and pleasurable activities. And if excess choice reduces consumer purchases, then the plethora of choices on the Internet could reduce rather than increase sales for firms.

Why do too many choices lead to choice paralysis? Researchers have proposed three explanations based on regret, anxiety, and effort. According to the regret explanation, having a lot of choice makes it easy for us to imagine that our selected option is worse than the options not chosen. For example, we may think fondly about the flavors of jam or ice cream passed over, the faster car forgone, or the hotel room with the better view rejected. One way to avoid this regret would be to simply not choose, since there are no forgone options if there is no choice. It doesn't help that review websites often highlight the top product in every category: best hotel, best laptop, best TV, and best family sedan. If we haven't chosen one of these top-rated products, it is easy to feel that we have made a mistake. Of course, "best" is often a subjective judgment and what is best for others may not be right for us. But we often don't see it that way and postpone choices to avoid being stuck with a subop-timal product.

Another way to avoid regret is to choose after so much delibera-tion that we can tell ourselves we have chosen the best option. Put-ting aside the value of lost time and the impracticality of thinking about every decision in painstaking detail, there is a hidden cost to ruminating about choices. Research has shown that thinking about choice options creates a sense of attachment towards all the con-sidered options, which makes it difficult to pick only one. Imagine you are shopping for a new car and have narrowed your choices to three brands: Mini Cooper, Mazda Miata, and Fiat 500. The more you think about these cars – each with its unique design, quirky personality, and glowing user reviews – the more painful it will be to choose only one, since this implies you must give up the other two cars to which you have become psychologically attached. In this way thinking about choices can make choosing feel like losing (Carmon, Wertenbroch, & Zeelenberg, 2003).

Another explanation for choice paralysis is that too much infor-mation creates anxiety, and one way to reduce this anxiety is to avoid choice altogether. Product packaging, especially in the case of food and medicine, often lists both positive information about product benefits and negative information about harmful ingredi-ents or side effects. As the amount of package information increases, the amount of negative information also increases, which can create anxiety during choice. I observed this anxiety effect in a research study where I showed two versions of food packaging to consumers (Hansen, Mukherjee, & Uth Thomsen, 2011). The packages differed in terms of nutritional information – some packages had a long list of ingredients including fat content, calories, vitamins, minerals, food coloring, preservatives, stabilizers, and flavoring agents, while others had a shorter list of main ingredients. I found that those who saw packages with more detailed information reported feeling more anxious, suggesting that exposure to more product information can create anxiety during choice.

Trade-off difficulty is another reason for anxiety during choice. We often make trade-offs – sacrificing our waistline for the melt-in-your-mouth taste of a Krispy Kreme donut; lower quality for the lower price of a second-hand car; or lesser environmental friendliness for the greater effectiveness of a harsh household cleaner. These trade-offs can create anxiety, since we are often unsure about whether we are making the right sacrifice for the right gain. Some trade-offs are especially difficult – think about giving up safety features for a cheaper car, or choosing a more effective heart medication with a chance of serious side effects. With such trade-offs, there are substantial risks in the form of lower safety or harmful side effects, which can create anxiety. Postponing choice allows us to avoid trade-off anxiety, since there are no difficult trade-offs to be made if there is no choice.

Researchers have used a brain imaging technique called fMRI – functional magnetic resonance imagery – to demonstrate that too much information creates anxiety during choice. fMRI machines use magnetic fields to measure blood flow and activation in different regions of the brain associated with feelings, thoughts, and behavior. One fMRI study investigated the effect of excess information while choosing by measuring brain activity during combinatorial auctions (Dimoka, 2010). Combinatorial auctions are complex bidding wars where many options can be bought separately or bundled together, such as airline landing slots being bid for by airlines. The challenge is to buy the combination of options you want at the lowest price, which is a difficult task if you are considering, say, 100 landing slots at the Toronto airport. As the number of options increases, the amount of information that bidders must juggle increases exponentially – passenger load, weather, and connecting flights – which makes the bidding process very complex.

Participants in this study were asked to bid in combinatorial auctions for airline landing slots while their brain activity was scanned by an fMRI machine. When the auction started, there was increased activity in the dorsolateral prefrontal cortex, the region of the brain responsible for rational decision-making. As the auction proceeded and information piled up, activity in this region dropped off and instead, regions of the brain related to emotion lit up. It was as if a circuit breaker had tripped due to a surge of anxiety and, when this happened, participants took longer to make decisions and started overpaying for options worth far less. Our brains misfire with negative emotion when we are overwhelmed by too much information, and our decisions suffer as a result.

A third explanation for choice paralysis is that people are "cognitive misers," looking to reduce mental effort during decision-making (Bettman, Luce, & Payne, 1998). We are receiving information all the time from our surroundings – social conversations, traffic, television, email, telephone, text messages, books, music, newspapers, and websites. This information is constantly changing and arriving through different channels of perception: sight, sound, taste, smell, and touch. We would need a supercomputer in our heads to thoroughly process all this information and make optimal decisions on a moment-to-moment basis. Instead, our minds often simplify matters by postponing choices that require too much thinking. This is akin to triage in hospitals – since doctors cannot see everyone at once, they keep some patients waiting to focus on others with more serious symptoms. Similarly, our minds keep some choices on hold to allocate limited mental resources to more important tasks. The California jam study discussed earlier is a good example of this process – most shoppers walked away without buying anything because it was simply too much effort to compare 24 different brands, flavors, and sizes before buying something as mundane as a jar of jam.

## Choice Shortcuts

People often navigate the world of excess information by using choice shortcuts. When we see a wall of ice cream at the grocery store, we can cut through the clutter by going straight to our favorite brand and flavor. When shopping for detergent or toilet paper, we use shortcuts such as buying the brand most familiar to us or the brand we bought last time. Research has found that people often use brand names as choice shortcuts, especially in markets with many competing brands (Hoyer & Brown, 1990). From Levi Strauss in the nineteenth century to Apple today, familiar brand names have always served as a badge of quality and a shortcut to choice. This is why firms spend heavily on branding and jealously guard their brand equity – brands bind customers with invisible chains of assurance and convenience in a world of excess information.

Food is an especially important choice because we all need to eat, and food choices have implications for health, household budgets, and personal well-being. How do people make food choices? What kinds of shortcuts do people use when buying food? I investigated these questions in a study where I presented consumers with two packages of frozen dinner: one package had a fictional health certification called "Heart Healthy" stamped on it, while the other package did not (Mukherjee, 2017). I simply asked participants to look at the two packages and pick the one they liked more. Not surprisingly, most participants in the study picked the "Heart Healthy" dinner. I then wondered if choosing on the basis of health certifications like "Heart Healthy" could hurt consumers, perhaps by making them overlook harmful product information on the package. So I modified the "Heart Healthy" packaging by adding unhealthy ingredients such as trans fat, preservatives, and stabilizers. Surprisingly I found this made no difference, with most people still picking the product with the prominent health certification despite the fact that it now had several harmful ingredients. It seems that consumers use the choice shortcut of prominent information on the label rather than detailed information at the back of the package, and this choice shortcut can mislead customers into making bad food choices.

Another common shortcut is to choose products on the basis of reviews posted by others on websites such as Yelp, TripAdvisor, or CNET. A majority of consumers around the world now consult product reviews before making purchase decisions, and this number has been increasing over time (Nielsen, 2015). There is an important problem with reviews, however, which is that different reviewers often have different opinions about the very same product. If you look up movie reviews on Rotten Tomatoes, you will see that many movies have mixed reviews: some people like them, others hate them, and yet others are in the middle. How can we use reviews when they are all over the place? Should we focus on the positives, the negatives, or the neutrals? One way people solve this problem is to look only at the average rating and ignore the variance in ratings across reviewers. Another common approach is to rely on one's "favorite reviewers" and ignore the others. These favorite reviewers are sometimes called opinion leaders, and research shows that people choose opinion leaders in different ways. We sometimes choose opinion leaders based on expertise, such as when we take the advice of professional critics for movies, music, or restaurants. At other times, we pick opinion leaders based on popularity, such as the number of likes or thumbs-up from other consumers. And we sometimes pick opinion leaders based on perceived similarity, such as movie reviewers who most resemble us in terms of age, gender, or education.

As with any choice shortcut, relying on opinion leaders can sometimes lead us astray. I learned this the hard way because I love watching movies and often seek out recommendations from friends, family, and online reviewers. I realized after many disappointments that recommendations are tricky – just because someone insists that I must see a movie doesn't mean I will like it. Others I talked to also said the same thing, namely that their favorite reviewers sometimes let them down by recommending bad or mediocre movies. When I discussed this issue with my research collaborators, we had an idea – perhaps people use a flawed method to select their favorite reviewer, and this makes recommendations from favorite reviewers less useful. To explore this issue, we conducted a study where we asked students in our classes to consider two movie reviewers, say John and Paul (Gershoff, Mukherjee, & Mukhopadhyay, 2007). We told students to imagine that John matched them on previously liked movies, while Paul matched them on previously disliked movies. As a concrete example, John was said to have liked the same 20 movies as them, while Paul had disliked the same 20 movies as them. We then asked students to pick either John or Paul as their preferred movie reviewer. We found that most students picked John as their preferred reviewer, indicating that the students were using a choice shortcut of picking the reviewer who had been good at predicting their past likes. Of course, this shortcut would backfire when it is more important for the reviewer to predict our dislikes. For example, when many mediocre or bad movies are being released, reviewers' main job is to steer us away from movies we would dislike. Another situation where this shortcut can backfire is when our tastes evolve over time, and we no longer like the movies that we liked in the past.

So far we have seen that people use familiar brands, health certifications, and opinion leaders as choice shortcuts in a world of excess information. Other shortcuts are also widely used during choice. For example, people often choose between similar options by selecting a dissimilar, albeit inferior, option (Redelmeier & Shafir, 1995); selecting a neutral option (Nowlis, Khan, & Dhar, 2002); selecting the option described as having more features (Shafir, Simonson, & Tversky, 1993); or selecting the option that is easiest to justify to others (Sela, Berger, & Liu, 2009). When choosing the amount of food to put on their plate, people use shortcuts such as the size of their plate, amount of food taken by others at their table, and the body weight of diners at surrounding tables (McFerran, Dahl, Fitzsimons, & Morales, 2010). The larger the plate, the more food others at the table are eating, and the heavier the surrounding diners, the more food we are likely to put on our own plates. These shortcuts during food choice are dangerous because they represent mindless rather than mindful eating, which could lead to weight gain and health problems over time.

People use shortcuts when searching for online information on Google or Bing. When we type in a search term, the results are ranked with the more relevant websites – according to the search engine – displayed on top. Research has found that people focus mainly on the top-ranked search results and largely ignore the rest. In one study, researchers asked voters in the 2014 national elections in India to google information about three politicians (Epstein & Robertson, 2015). Different groups of voters were shown different search results – the top-ranked results in the first group linked to web pages favorable to the first politician, while the top-ranked results in the second and third groups favored the second and third politician respectively. It turned out that voters' opinion of politicians was determined almost entirely by the top-ranked results. This was especially true of uncommitted voters, and these voters also expressed a higher intention to vote for the politician with top-ranked results. Closely fought elections in many countries are decided by uncommitted voters. If uncommitted voters use search shortcuts rather than thoughtful analysis to make voting decisions, the democratic process can be subverted by candidates who have optimized their search ranking over those who have a better agenda for the country.

An important effect of choice shortcuts is that they entrench the dominance of big brands in the marketplace. Despite the thousands of new movies released every year, the lion's share of movie profits are made by a few heavily promoted blockbusters and sequels that rely on name recognition to sell tickets. For example, there were 558 films released in North America during 2009, most of which failed to make a profit; this was also the year when *Avatar* became the highest grossing film to date. Franchises like *Superman*, *Spiderman*, *Avengers*, and *Star Trek* are moneymakers because many people use a well-known franchise, movie star, or movie award as a shortcut for deciding what to watch at the multiplex. As a result, brands with high awareness – because they have been successful in the past, present in the market for a long time, or advertised more heavily – are likely to have an inherent advantage in a world of excess information.

## Post-Choice Dissatisfaction

Too much information can lead to "buyer's remorse" or post-choice dissatisfaction, where we end up regretting the choice we just made (Iyengar & Lepper, 2000). This is indicated by surveys showing that up to 40 percent of shoppers experience regret about a recently purchased product (Freeman, Spenner, & Bird, 2012). Why might we feel buyer's remorse? One reason is that the more information we gather online about the products and services we own, the more likely it is that we will find other brands that look more attractive than ours in terms of features or price. This will make our own purchases look inferior in comparison and create feelings of dissatisfaction.

Another reason for buyer's remorse is that too much information increases hedonic adaptation (Frederick & Loewenstein, 1999). Hedonic adaptation is our tendency to discount the value of things we have, compared to things we don't have. This is why newly introduced versions of the iPhone or Xbox devalue the perfectly good versions of these products we currently own. And the more new products we see online, the more quickly we devalue the products we own. Too much information can also reduce post-choice satisfaction through exposure to negative word of mouth about the products we own. If we read reviews on CNET or Yelp about the new computer we just bought, we are likely to find at least a few negative reviews from other users. Since people have a tendency to focus more on negative than positive information, even a few negative reviews might convince us that the product we just bought is of inferior quality (Chan & Cui, 2011).

## Barriers to Learning

People generally believe that more information is better than less; after all, that's what they teach in school. But surprisingly, research shows that having easy access to lots of information can actually hinder our ability to learn. There are three reasons for this paradox: delegation of memory, memory biases, and memory scaffolding. We often delegate memory to other people, such as when we ask our partner to remember birthdays of friends and family while we take responsibility for paying the bills on time. Similarly, we have now started delegating our memory to the Internet by relying on Google Drive, Dropbox, Facebook, and Wikipedia rather than information in our own minds (Sparrow & Chatman, 2013). On one hand, it makes sense to rely on the Internet because there is virtually no limit on storage capacity, and information can be easily accessed with search engines. Relying on information from the Internet is also helpful because it lets us focus on creative tasks rather than rote memorization. On the other hand, relying on the Internet atrophies our ability to learn since we now make less effort to organize and understand information in our own mind. Because we no longer make an effort to mentally digest, we lose the ability to transform raw information into knowledge. This "Google effect" on memory was shown in a study (Sparrow, Liu, & Wegner, 2011) where participants were asked to copy 40 memorable statements into a computer (e.g., "An ostrich's eye is bigger than its head"). Half of the participants were told that the information they were transcribing would be available online indefinitely, while the other half were told that the information would later be deleted. Participants were later asked to recall as many of the 40 sentences as they could. The researchers found that those who believed their work was being saved online were worse at remembering the sentences later than were those who thought their work would be deleted. The more we rely on the Internet to remember things for us, the worse we are at remembering things ourselves.

The surfeit of information online can bias our memories of facts and events. A well-known memory bias is the familiarity-truth effect, as expressed in the saying "repeat a lie a thousand times and it becomes the truth." This is why firms sometimes pay people to post false positive reviews about their products on review websites. Consumers who repeatedly see positive reviews will come away with the impression that the reviews are probably true and the product in question works well. The familiarity-truth effect also explains why rumors become stronger when they go viral on the Internet – people mistakenly believe that something they read many times on the Internet must ipso facto be true.

The power of rumors is further enhanced by another memory bias called the sleeper effect. This is the tendency for people to remember something they heard longer than the identity of the person who said it. In other words, people remember claims better than the person who makes the claims. Because of the sleeper effect, even claims made by unreliable or unknown people on the Internet can take on the patina of truth over time because people tend to forget that they heard the claim from an unreliable source in the first place.

Our memories can be biased by the speed with which search results are served up on search engines: the quicker search results are delivered, the more knowledgeable people think they are about the topics in question. This was shown in a study where people took part in a trivia quiz (Galinsky, Ku, & Wang, 2005). One group of participants completed the quiz without the help of the Internet, while the other group was allowed to use the Internet to find answers to their questions. Participants were then asked to state how knowledgeable they felt about the topics in the quiz. The researchers found that people who completed the quiz using the Internet felt more confident about their knowledge of the topics in the quiz than did those without Internet access. Furthermore, people who overestimated their knowledge also predicted that they would do better in a second quiz without help from the Internet. This study suggests that merely having access to the Internet is enough to make us feel smarter, even though we may not actually be an expert on the topic in the absence of the Internet. Interestingly, this overconfidence bias seems to increase with faster Internet access. In a follow-up study, the researchers found that broadband users with fast Internet access were more confident about their knowledge than users of slower dial-up Internet. Faster Internet access – and hence a shorter waiting period – gives people less time to think about their actual knowledge and strengthens the illusion that information on the Internet is knowledge we possess in our brains.

Yet another drawback of keeping information on the Internet is that it removes the memory scaffolding required for learning. When we are trying to learn new things – be it cooking, music, languages, or mathematics – we need to first erect a basic framework of knowledge and then add new information around this framework. This "framework-first" approach is as true for learning as it is for building a house or a bridge: the framework provides the skeleton, which is then fleshed out into a complete structure. Keeping information externally on the Internet rather than in our minds leaves us without the internal knowledge skeleton we need to assimilate new information effectively. As a result, outsourcing information to the Internet can undermine our ability to learn.

## What Can We Do?

We can take three steps to minimize the negative effects of too much information on the Internet: satisfice rather than maximize, delegate choice, and use decision tools.

### Satisfice, Don't Maximize

The message we constantly get from society and the world of advertising is that we should aim for the best – the biggest house, the most prestigious job, the fanciest vacations, and the best car. Of course it is good to be ambitious, but aiming for the best all the time might be counterproductive when making choices in life. Broadly speaking, we can approach life with either a maximization goal, where we seek to make the best possible choice, or a "satisficing" goal, where we are satisfied with a "good enough" choice. Research shows that having a maximizing goal during choice increases post-purchase regret and reduces satisfaction with the products we choose (Schwartz et al., 2002). In this research, people first filled out a questionnaire that measured the extent to which they were maximizers or satisficers. People then reported their regret about recent product purchases as well as their overall happiness with life. The researchers found that maximizers expressed more regret and lower life satisfaction than satisficers.

Another study found that maximizers feel worse about their decisions than satisficers even when they make objectively better decisions (Iyengar, Wells, & Schwartz, 2006). This study followed graduating college students during their job search process and subsequent working life. Students who were maximizers did better initially in terms of getting a higher starting salary, but they fared significantly worse later in terms of job satisfaction. Why did this happen? One reason could be that maximizers focus on quantifiable things such as money and prestige when choosing careers, at the cost of things that are less quantifiable but more important in the long run, such as job satisfaction and social impact. Perhaps we might be better off adopting a satisficing approach towards many of our daily choices and reserving a maximizing goal for only a few important choices. Even for these important choices, it might make sense to use a satisficing approach for shortlisting an initial set of options, and then switch to a maximizing mindset for making the final choice. There is a lot of wisdom in the saying "don't sweat the small stuff, and it's mostly small stuff."

## Delegate Choice

We can manage excess information by delegating choice. We normally think about choice as a comparison of brands and their features, followed by selection of the best brand. But we could also think about choice more broadly in terms of when to choose versus when not to choose; when to let others choose for us; how many alternatives to consider; and how much time to spend on the decision-making process. When the decision is highly complex, we could let experts like doctors and lawyers make decisions for us. We could routinize regular decisions such as what to wear for work by adopting a standard look for each day of the week – if it's Monday, it must be blue shirt with red tie, black turtleneck with jeans on Tuesday, and so on. We could set up rules in advance that simplify decision-making in the grocery store, such as "consider no more than two brands in each product category, and make a decision within 10 seconds." We should not look at grocery flyers after we have finished shopping because then we might learn that we should have bought something else or shopped somewhere else. These techniques will help us by delegating choices to other people or to automatic rules set up in advance.

## Decision Tools

We can improve our choices by using decision tools. Wine stores often publish notes to educate buyers about the taste profiles of wines and suggested food pairings. These tasting notes are decision tools – tools to help us better understand what we like and dislike. Decision tools are especially important for products like wine, a market where people are relatively uninformed and don't know what to look for (Hoeffler, 2003). A particularly useful preference learning tool available in the form of software is called conjoint analysis (Ding, Grewal, & Liechty, 2005). Imagine you are thinking of buying a new home. If you use conjoint analysis software, you will be asked to choose between homes with different combinations of features, say a more expensive home with more bedrooms versus a less expensive home with fewer bedrooms; or a larger home with a longer commute time versus a smaller home with a shorter commute time. As you can see, these choices represent trade-offs between different features – price, number of bedrooms, floor area, and commute time. The trade-offs you make through your choices are analyzed by the software to quantify which features of homes you value more and which less. Your choices will also reveal the ideal combination of features and price that is your personal "sweet spot" for a home. Armed with this precise knowledge about your own preferences, you can proceed to buy the home which is right for you, one that satisfies both your heart and your wallet.

Product filtering tools can be an effective ally against too much information. Travel websites such as Expedia allow us to filter airline tickets by price or flight connections so that we see only options below a certain price or with fewer than a certain number of connections. These filters reduce the number of options we need to consider, thus reducing information overload during choice. Similarly, websites that compare multiple brands and features on the screen at the same time simplify choices by making it easier to compare options side-by-side on features important to us. We could use recommendation agents such as those offered by Amazon or Netflix that give suggestions based on our past history of purchases and the purchases of those similar to us. When we are unsure about what to buy, we could save time and effort by simply accepting suggestions from recommendation agents. Indeed, research shows that using recommendation agents reduces search effort, increases decision quality, and increases satisfaction with choice (Dellaert & Häubl, 2012). And finally, using recommendation agents can lead to serendipitous discoveries of new movies, books, or music that we might never have come across had we stuck to our past pattern of choices.

# TOO MUCH CUSTOMIZATION

If you want to buy a Daihatsu Copen car in Japan, you can choose from one of 15 "effect skins," decorative panels with intricate patterns in different colors. You can arrange these panels to create the look you want, and your custom car will be printed using thermoplastic materials on 3D printers (Print My Ride, 2016). Not just cars, we can customize many other products and services online. Jimmy Choo allows customers to create their own shoes by mixing and matching different styles, heights, and colors. If you've been to a McDonald's lately, you'll have noticed the touchscreen terminals where consumers can create custom meals by selecting their favorite filling, bread, toppings, fries, and drinks. The Internet has made it easy for consumers to tailor products to their unique tastes and preferences.

Firms can also use the Internet to customize advertising, product recommendations, and product offerings. Google's business model is based on serving up advertising relevant to our recent online behavior. Facebook tailors advertising to our personal profiles, social media postings, and behavior of our online friends, while Amazon and Netflix use algorithms to make individualized recommendations for books, movies, and music. In the past, firms could not afford to stock too many types of products in stores because of the high cost of manufacturing, inventory, and distribution associated with product variety. Now, with 3D printing, online ordering, and just-in-time inventory, firms can offer a huge variety of products online at competitive prices. This growth of product customization on the Internet is sometimes called the "long tail" effect, which refers to the ever-extending "tail" or variety of products being offered by firms online (Anderson, 2006).

The ability to customize is helpful in many ways. The more we can customize a product, the more likely it is that it will fit our unique needs and wants. Customized advertising should be more useful to us than mass advertising because the advertised product is something we are interested in. In fact, Facebook encourages users to set their ad preferences so that only advertising for personally relevant products is shown to them. Customized pricing on travel websites such as Expedia can lead to lower prices as a reward for past customer loyalty. In a win-win, customized pricing is also good for firms; research indicates that firms offering customized prices reap higher profits, especially when there are opportunities to add new services to the offering (Acquisti & Varian, 2005). Other research has shown that online advertising tailored to customer behavior attracts more attention than generic advertising (Hauser, Urban, Liberali, & Braun, 2009), and customization of Web interfaces to user preferences increases browsing time and customer satisfaction (Chung, Wedel, & Rust, 2016).

Although online customization can benefit both customers and firms, what is less well known is that customization can also hurt us in a number of ways. In particular, research shows that customization can have negative effects in terms of attitude formation, creativity, risky behavior, product attachment, product assembly, product co-creation, product pricing, and online advertising.

## Attitude Formation

We often form our attitudes about products and people when we go online. Every time we see an online advertisement for a smartphone, a customer review of a hotel, or a news article about a politician, our attitude towards the product or person in question is influenced one way or the other. An important bias during this attitude formation process is the "echo chamber effect" (Jasny, Waggle, & Fisher, 2015). Just as echo chambers reflect our own voice back to us, the Internet creates an echo chamber that reflects and reinforces our existing attitudes. Suppose you have a strong conviction – say global warming is a hoax, household cleaning products are carcinogenic, nefarious people are conspiring against your kind, or vaccines lead to autism. Chances are that you can easily find support for these or any other belief on the Internet simply by googling relevant search terms. The sheer number of people online makes it likely, statistically, that supportive posts for beliefs held by even a small percentage of the population can be found on the Internet. Improvements in search technology also mean that it is now easier to find information we are looking for online. For example, we will get very different perspectives on the same issue depending on whether we search for #ACA and #BlackLivesMatter, compared to #Obamacare and #AllLivesMatter. The Internet makes it easy to segregate ourselves into echo chambers, each sealed off from the other and populated with like-minded people who simply reinforce our existing opinions.

The echo chamber effect gets its power from a psychological process called confirmation bias. Confirmation bias is the tendency people have to remember, think, and act in a manner consistent with their preexisting beliefs and attitudes. For example, researchers have found that people are more likely to remember good things about products they like and bad things about products they dislike (Hoch & Deighton, 1989). Similarly, we are more likely to remember positive news reports about products we have already bought – and hence presumably like – compared to products we have not purchased yet (Mukherjee & Hoyer, 2001). Pharmaceutical companies have long known that inert pills described as medicine are often highly effective if patients think they are receiving real medication

(Shiv, Carmon, & Ariely, 2005). The reason for this so-called placebo effect is that patients generally believe medicines work, especially when administered by white-coated doctors in a clinical setting. So when we are given a pill described as medicine – even if it is actually an inert pill – our minds interpret random health benefits that occur by chance as evidence of the pill's efficacy. A useful analogy for confirmation bias is that prior beliefs create a pathway in the mind, and our subsequent memories, thoughts, and actions tend to follow this path.

The echo chamber effect is really the confirmation bias on steroids: our minds seek confirmation, and the Internet makes it easy to surround ourselves with consistent information. This is ironic because the Internet actually offers an unprecedented range of opinions and perspectives from around the world. Unfortunately, this variety is filtered through the distorting lens of our mind's confirmation bias, which prevents us from appreciating alternative viewpoints. If we wanted to, we could browse online newspapers with political views different from ours, watch movies different from what we normally see, and listen to any genre of music outside our usual style. But how many of us actually do so? Although our options have expanded, our ability to customize has too, and this allows us to live within the silo of our existing preferences.

Confirmation bias also explains the power of fake news as a propaganda tool. The US presidential election of 2016 saw the weapons-grade use of fake news to influence public opinion. From hackers in the Kremlin and fly-by-night websites in Macedonia came sensational but untrue stories of Hillary Clinton's pedophile connections and Barack Obama saying that Americans deserved to be attacked on 9/11. You may laugh but people clicked on these articles by the millions. In fact, a news analysis by Buzz-Feed found that during the last three months of the 2016 US presidential election, fake election news on Facebook outperformed real news from sources like the *New York Times* on every measure of engagement – clicks, likes, shares, and comments. Facebook's algorithms further magnify the effect of fake news by prioritizing content in line with what you, or people you know, have clicked, liked, or shared in the past. In this way, Facebook acts as an amplifier of the echo chamber effect. Fake news is most influential when it feeds into existing beliefs, confirming dislike for enemies and cementing affections for friends. As such, fake news finds the most fertile ground in a divided electorate with clear in-groups and out-groups, where people are ready to accept statements without normal standards of proof so long as the claims are consistent with what they already believe in. And the more fake news is forwarded, retweeted, and commented on online, the more credible it becomes through the power of repetition.

The echo chamber effect is now spreading from the online to the offline world. Census data suggests that people are increasingly clustering in neighborhoods and cities dominated by people with similar political, religious, and social views. This combination of online and offline clustering will strengthen the echo chamber effect by ensuring that we are rarely exposed to views that contradict our existing opinions. Even worse, uniformity of information is likely to make us more confident and extreme in our views over time. This is bad news at an individual level because it effectively closes our minds to different points of view. This is also harmful at a broader social level because a polarized country which cannot give a fair hearing to opposite points of view will become politically paralyzed, with each faction being convinced of the superiority of its own cause.

## Creativity

Creativity is the ability to "think outside the box," that is, being able to come up with novel ideas outside the conventional range of options (Dahl & Moreau, 2007). One reason why children are often creative in ways adults are not is that they can let their imaginations run riot. As we grow up, many factors conspire to narrow our thinking – education systems that reward right answers rather than novel answers, social circumstances that favor safety over experimentation, and our increased ability to customize the online environment. These factors, together with our inbuilt confirmation bias, progressively narrow our perspectives on issues and ideas. The narrower the range of information we see on a daily basis, the more we train our minds to think in a restricted range rather than consider "out-of-the-box" possibilities. Over time, this process will reduce our creativity and make it more difficult for us to come up with breakthrough ideas. This will also retard our growth as individuals because going outside our comfort zone is what forces us to reflect and add new layers to our personality.

## Risky Behavior

The ability to customize can increase risky financial behavior. The Internet has given us more control over our finances by letting us monitor investments on a daily basis and make complex financial trading decisions that could earlier be executed only by professionals. An unintended consequence of putting such tools in the hands of lay investors is that control over the process of investing can lead people to assume they have control over investment outcomes as well. For example, many investors use online dashboards to track market metrics such as stock prices, historical trends, and financial news. Having access to all this information could give investors a false sense of confidence that they have everything they need to beat the market and make winning investments. Of course, the truth is that stock prices are virtually impossible for lay investors to forecast with any degree of accuracy. But the illusion of control created by online tools can encourage risky financial decisions that put our savings at risk.

The illusion of control over financial decisions is just one example of a more general human tendency to assume more control over their environment than is warranted by the facts. For example, studies have shown that gamblers assume they have greater control over the outcome of a die throw if they personally throw the dice compared to someone else throwing it for them (Taylor & Brown, 1988). Similar illusions of control have been observed in card games and lotteries where outcomes are actually determined by chance but people assume they can influence the outcome by choosing "lucky" numbers. The ability to customize on the Internet can magnify this illusion of control, leading to risky financial decisions and losses in the stock market.

## Product Attachment

Let's return to the example of customizing a car on the Internet. Research on the endowment effect suggests that customization can increase the price people are willing to pay for the car. The endowment effect is the idea that ownership, or even imagined ownership, of a product makes it seem more valuable (Kahneman, Knetsch, & Thaler 1990; Peck & Shu, 2009). This effect was illustrated in a study where researchers showed a coffee mug to two groups of people (Kahneman et al., 1990). One group was asked to state the maximum price at which they would be willing to buy the mug. The other group was told that the mug was theirs to keep and then asked to state the minimum price at which they would be willing to sell the mug. Supporting the endowment effect, it was found that the average selling price – from people who thought the mug was theirs to keep – was more than double the average buying price quoted by people who simply looked at the mug. In a different study, it was found that actual ownership is not required for the endowment effect, and the effect also emerges when people imagine they own a product or even when they simply touch a product (Peck & Shu, 2009).

Customizing products can induce a sense of ownership by making it easy to imagine that the product is already in our possession. This sense of virtual ownership or virtual endowment will increase the price we are willing to pay for a customized product. The increased price of customized products, in turn, can create higher expectations of performance. For example, we expect a pricier car to be more reliable and quieter than a less expensive car. These higher expectations for expensive products, however, can be a double-edged sword. Research on customer satisfaction shows that high expectations are good if the product performs at or above expectations, but the same high expectations can set us up for disappointment if the product malfunctions in even small ways (Szymanski & Henard, 2001). Thus the car we spend a lot of time customizing will carry a heavy burden of inflated expectations, and even small problems that inevitably arise during ownership will loom large, leading to eventual disappointment with our choice.

## Product Assembly

Another situation where customization can backfire is during product assembly. Consumers often assemble products and services from their component parts. We design vacations online by combining bookings for hotels, flights, excursions, and restaurant meals; we create online art with a virtual palette of materials; and we play online games where our goal is to create virtual worlds with people, buildings, money, and armies. Research has shown that the ability to customize during product assembly can influence perceived value of the product, depending on the nature of the customization task

(Buechel & Janiszewski, 2014). To study this issue, the researchers asked participants to work on a craft project where the objective was to create a decorative figure of a winter elf by cutting out adornment pieces (e.g., ears, mittens, shoes) from holiday wrapping paper and pasting the adornments onto an outline of an elf. After completing the assembly task, participants were asked to estimate the value of the craft kit used to create the elf.

The researchers found that peoples' valuation of the craft kit depended on whether the customization and assembly phases of the task occurred together or separately. When customization and assembly occurred together (i.e., when participants were told to cut out an adornment they liked and immediately paste it into the outline of the elf), their valuation of the kit was high. In contrast, when customization and assembly was segregated (i.e., when participants were told to first cut out all the adornments they liked and only later to start the process of pasting them onto the elf), valuation of the kit was reduced. The likely reason for these results is that customization is a creative process that people enjoy, but the act of assembly is a more mechanical and tedious task. So when people do customization and assembly at the same time, positive feelings from customization compensate for negative feelings from assembly. However, when these two tasks are done separately, the later assembly task stands out as a separate and more recent negative event that reduces overall valuation of the product.

This study has implications for products such as online craft projects and multiplayer games that involve creation in a virtual world. Designers of such products should ensure that users can customize and assemble at the same time, rather than at different points in time. Similarly, online travel websites should encourage users to select and arrange their itineraries simultaneously, rather than at different times. In the offline world, this research suggests that the Ikea approach – select components in the store and assemble them later at home – may not be the best strategy, since the separate assembly phase at home could create negative feelings about Ikea.

## Product Co-creation

Firms sometimes ask consumers to submit ideas for products and services online, with the best ideas being used later by firms to develop new offerings. Such product co-creation between firms and consumers is a type of customization, because products are being tailored to specifications received from consumers. Research has shown that product co-creation can backfire for luxury products such as designer clothes, shoes, and handbags (Fuchs, Prandelli, Schreier, & Dahl, 2013). This is because the value of luxury products is undercut when these products are known to be based on inputs from regular people, rather than professional designers. Product co-creation works better in the case of products intended for everyday use. For example, firms sometimes organize contests to pick the brand name for a new type of yogurt or the flavor of a new line of potato chips, and research suggests this type of product co-creation is likely to be more successful. Firms offering luxury products, in contrast, should use the services of professional designers rather than inputs from lay customers when designing new products.

## Product Pricing

Pricing is yet another area where customization can have negative effects (Kannan, Pope, & Jain, 2009). Modern retailing replaced haggling in bazaars and souks by introducing the price tag featuring a single price for everyone. Merchants like Roland Macy and John

Wannamaker opened the first department stores in the nineteenth century with the principle "one price to all: no favoritism." But eventually prices started varying because retailers understood that everyone likes a good deal and some customers are more willing to pay a higher price than others. Thus price customization became common for airlines, hotels, sporting events, and car parking. The basic idea in price customization is to charge different prices to different customers at different times, depending on how much the customer in question values the product. For example, airlines often charge higher prices during peak travel times; parking spots are more expensive during the day than in the evening; Uber uses surge pricing on Saturday nights when demand for a ride is high; Coca-Cola has experimented with charging more for a can of Coke on hot days when demand for a cold drink is high; and people living in affluent urban neighborhoods are sometimes quoted higher prices by online retailers than those living in more remote areas.

Although price customization might make economic sense by matching prices to demand, customers sometimes resent having to pay a higher price for the exact same product. This is especially true in markets with less competition, where customers have fewer alternatives if they refuse to buy the product being offered at a customized price (Xia, Monroe, & Cox, 2004). In the long run, customers who think that a firm is being unfair to them in terms of price are defectors-in-waiting, ready to jump ship to a competing firm as soon as a reasonable alternative becomes available.

## Online Advertising

Customization is becoming increasingly common in online advertising. Advertising platforms such as Google and Facebook harvest information about our online activities using cookies in our computers, our IP addresses, and the information we post on social media. This information is then used to serve up advertisements that closely match our recent browsing behavior or recent events in our lives. Try searching on Google for a vacation in Jamaica and then observe the ads that pop up. Chances are that you will find at least some of these ads to be for vacation- and travel-related products and services.

A danger with such targeted advertising is that it can easily fall into the "uncanny valley." Uncanny valley is a term coined by roboticist Masahiro Mori to describe the revulsion people experience when seeing robots that look and act almost, but not exactly, like human beings (Mori, MacDorman, & Kageki, 2012). Advertising that is highly customized to our past behavior can make us feel uncomfortable by giving us the feeling that we are being intelligently followed by technology that is clearly not human.

Customization also happens when we look for information on search engines. Search engines often have access to our search history, that is, the things we have searched for and clicked on in the past. This information is used by the search engine algorithm to generate results judged to be most relevant to us. This kind of personalization can create an incestuous loop: we are shown results that match our existing preferences, which further strengthens those very preferences. In this way, online search reinforces what we currently like or dislike and thereby limits the extension of our mental horizons.

## What Can We Do?

One way to reduce the echo chamber effect is by pre-committing to alternative points of view. For example, when we browse news on the Internet, we could establish a habit of alternating between different news sources – one with a political orientation that matches ours followed by one with an opposite orientation. Balancing news across the ideological spectrum will help us better understand the arguments supporting our current opinions and thus help us better debate others with different viewpoints. It would be useful to read discussion websites such as Quora, where people answer hot-button questions from different political, economic, and cultural perspectives. Just like Google has an "I'm feeling lucky" button, news feeds could include a "learn more" button that offers a different perspective on current issues. And one of the most fun ways to break out of the echo chamber is to travel widely. There is no substitute for personal experience, and travel will expose us to new ideas, lifestyles, and cultures in ways no website or book can.

Firms can benefit from customization by designing websites to fit their customers' information processing style. Research shows that people differ in whether they process information in a visual or a verbal manner (Wyer, Hung, & Jiang, 2008). People with a verbal style are good at processing symbolic information such as words and numbers, while those with a visual style are better at processing pictures and graphs. Firms often have the ability to present information on their websites in verbal or visual form. For example, financial services websites can show the same information either as numerical spreadsheets or pie charts, and fitness tracking software can show workout progress either in visual charts or numerical tables. Customers with a visual processing style will find it easier to absorb information from a visual interface, whereas those with a verbal processing style would benefit from a numerical or verbal interface. Firms could measure the information processing style of their customers using a short online questionnaire (Wyer et al., 2008), and then present either the verbal or visual version of their website to the customer.

Firms could customize their online advertising to the website on which the ad appears. Websites can be broadly classified as either social or commercial depending on their business objective. Those that facilitate connections between people (e.g., Facebook) are social;

those that focus on market exchanges (e.g., Amazon) are commercial (McGraw, Schwartz, & Tetlock, 2012). In one of my research projects (Auschaitrakul & Mukherjee, 2017), I studied the effectiveness of online advertising on social versus commercial websites. I asked people from an online research panel to read the mission statements of either Facebook or Amazon and then view a screen capture from one of these websites. As on real websites, the screen capture included online banner advertisements for products in different categories ranging from airlines to shoes. Participants in the study then rated their attitude towards each advertisement on a seven-point scale, with low numbers indicating dislike and high numbers indicating that they liked the ads. I found that people liked ads more when they saw them on a commercial website (e.g., Amazon) and less when they saw them on a social website (e.g., Facebook). The likely reason for this finding is that consumers expect a certain level of advertising on commercial websites but not on social websites, and hence they react negatively to advertising on social websites. The implication for firms is that online banner advertising is likely to be more effective on commercial websites than social websites.

In a follow-up study, I investigated whether the effectiveness of online advertising depends on the product benefit described in the ad. I focused on social websites (e.g., Facebook) in this study and found that advertising that emphasizes social benefits is more effective than advertising that emphasizes individual benefits. For example, advertisements for cars that highlighted social benefits such as having a good time with family and friends worked better on social websites than those emphasizing mileage and reliability. These results can be understood in terms of consistency between product benefit and the type of website: social benefits are more consistent with social websites and are thus more effective on these websites than individual benefits.

Finally, firms can help consumers navigate through the customization process by offering default options. For example, car or travel websites that require customers to choose from a menu of options could present a pre-selected default option at each stage of the customization process. Customers who are less informed about product features can move quickly through the selection process by simply accepting the default options. Other customers who are better informed would be free to reject the default options and proactively make their own unique selections.

# TOO MANY COMPARISONS

Social networks have made it easy to compare ourselves with others. More than a billion people now use Facebook, with the average user spending almost half an hour every day on this website. Besides Facebook, we also interact with people on other online platforms such as Twitter, Instagram, Pinterest, Periscope, and YouTube. The average Facebook user has more than 200 friends and, in addition, could be connected with many others on Twitter and Instagram. Contrast this with the relatively few people we had daily contact with before the Internet, and the limited knowledge we had about their lives. Online social networks have made it easier to stay in touch with friends and family around the world, but the dark side of social networks is that they can easily become a den of comparison.

As social animals, we are hardwired to compare ourselves with others. Other people provide a standard for judging ourselves and answering questions such as "Am I attractive? Am I smart? Am I successful?" In fact, research shows that many of our daily thoughts are about how we stack up against others (Summerville & Roese, 2008). It is not an accident that the celebrity fishbowl better known as the *National Enquirer* sells nearly three times as many copies as the more substantial *Atlantic* magazine. Online social networks have simply magnified this inherent aspect of human nature whereby we are programmed to compare ourselves to others. And beyond increased comparisons, online social networks have another important effect: they encourage upward rather than downward social comparisons on the Internet.

## Upward Social Comparisons

Upward social comparisons are comparisons where we focus on people who are better than us. For example, a student comparing his or her B grade with another student's A grade is using upward social comparison. In contrast, downward social comparison is when the same student compares his or her B grade with a student who got a lower grade, such as a C. Social networks like Facebook allow posters to pick and choose the personal information they want to share with others. One of the strongest human motives is self-enhancement, which is the drive to look good in the eyes of others. Because of this motive, people are more likely to post positive rather than negative or neutral information about themselves on social networks. This was confirmed in one of my research studies described earlier where I found that the vast majority of pictures posted on Facebook were of people having a good time (Auschaitrakul & Mukherjee, 2014). Similarly, even though the Las Vegas budget hotel Circus Circus and the luxury hotel Bellagio have about the same number of guests, the Bellagio gets more than three times the check-ins of Circus Circus on Facebook. We might send an unflattering selfie to close friends on Snapchat, but we are careful to post only beautiful vacation pictures for bigger audiences on Instagram or Facebook. People like to show off, and social media has given us a bigger stage and a brighter spotlight than ever before to flaunt our stuff.

Research has found that, compared to face-to-face communication, online communication prompts people to talk more about unusual and desirable products they own (Berger & Iyengar, 2013). This is because online communication is usually in written form while face-to-face communication is in oral form. Writing gives people the time to construct and refine what they want to say and, during this time, the self-enhancement motive drives people to come up with interesting things to post. And once people start posting interesting information, others are likely to follow suit in a bid to keep up with the Joneses. This creates an arms race of one-upmanship, leading to ever more upward social comparisons on the Internet. The size of the audience also makes a difference: when we are describing what we did to a large number of friends online, we are more likely to report positive experiences (Barasch & Berger, 2014). Given that most of us have hundreds of Facebook friends, this is a recipe for constant upward social comparisons online.

## Costs of Upward Social Comparisons

What are the psychological effects of upward social comparisons? I studied this question in a follow-up to the Facebook study described earlier (Auschaitrakul & Mukherjee, 2014). In this study, I asked half the participants to log in to their personal Facebook account and browse postings for 20 minutes; the remaining participants were asked to browse CNN for 20 minutes. All participants then completed a questionnaire measuring emotions such as pride, anger, joy, and envy. My goal in this study was to find out which emotions are most strongly associated with browsing social networks (e.g., Facebook) compared to other types of websites (e.g., CNN). Of all the emotions measured, I found that envy was most strongly associated with browsing social networks such as Facebook. Since envy is created by upward social comparisons (Festinger, 1954; Mussweiler, Rüter, & Epstude, 2004), this study suggests that browsing social networks often make us envious.

Of course, envy can be a good or bad thing. On the positive side, envy can motivate people to work hard to advance their social standing (Gershman, 2014; Wood, 1989). On the other hand, people experiencing envy are often ashamed and spend mental energy trying to conceal their feelings from others (van de Ven, Zeelenberg, & Pieters, 2009). As discussed earlier, expending mental energy reduces self-control, which often leads to decisions we regret later. Another negative effect of envy is that it creates a bad mood that can accumulate over time into a general dissatisfaction with life.

We have seen so far that social networks encourage upward social comparisons. We have also seen how feelings of envy from upward social comparisons can hurt us by increasing stress levels, lowering self-control, inducing a negative mood, and increasing dissatisfaction with life. Given these negative effects, it is fair to ask: Why do people engage in upward social comparisons? Why don't we simply stop comparing ourselves to others who are better off than us? The answer is that upward social comparisons are a powerful and instinctive human response, an ingrained way of thinking that is carved into our minds.

## Power of Upward Social Comparisons

There are four psychological reasons why upward social comparisons often dominate our thoughts: hedonic treadmill, hedonic adaptation, social norms, and evolution. As discussed in the first chapter, the hedonic treadmill is our tendency to revise ideal states upward over time to maintain a gap between ideal and actual states. The hedonic treadmill explains why it is challenging for firms to maintain high customer satisfaction over time. Customers soon get used to good service and, because of the hedonic treadmill, quickly start expecting more than what is currently being offered. For example, firms that reply to customer emails within hours soon find that customers begin to expect replies within minutes instead of hours. A folksy way of understanding the hedonic treadmill is the saying "the grass is always greener on the other side of the fence." Actually a more accurate version of this saying would be "the grass is always greener in the best backyard in our neighborhood." In other words, we compare our grass not with that of our immediate neighbors but with that of the neighbor who has the greenest grass. As new homes are built, the hedonic treadmill brings to mind the newest and best backyards with which to compare our own. The hedonic treadmill also implies that upward social comparisons never die – they are simply reborn in the form of new ideal states. No matter how successful we are and how many goals we have achieved, the hedonic treadmill raises the bar for how we define success in our own minds. And if we evaluate our life against the top 1 percent of our peers, we are setting ourselves up for feelings of inadequacy and failure.

Another psychological factor driving upward social comparisons is hedonic adaptation. We can understand hedonic adaptation through the same saying: "the grass is always greener." According to hedonic adaptation, our own grass starts appearing less green to our eyes over time. The longer we have something, the more we get used to it and the less we appreciate it. Hedonic adaptation was demonstrated in a research study where two groups of people were asked to rate their happiness in life: one group immediately after winning a million dollars in a lottery, and the other group after an accident that cost them the use of their legs (Brickman, Coates, & Janoff-Bulman, 1978). Not surprisingly, lottery winners rated their life happiness as being higher than accident victims. More surprisingly, when these two groups were followed up after a year, the gap between the groups on expressed life happiness had narrowed significantly. At this point, the lottery winners were still somewhat happier than the accident victims but not more so than people in general. Even more surprisingly, although the accident victims were somewhat less happy than people in general, they still judged themselves to be quite satisfied with their lot in life. Although lottery winners and the accident victims differ greatly in life circumstances, we can see that their life satisfaction is being driven less by the objective facts of their lives and more by hedonic adaptation to events. People adjusted to their condition, such that bad situations became tolerable and good situations became boring over time. People also changed their definition of a good life in a way that hurt or helped their life satisfaction: lottery winners visualized lifestyles of the rich and famous and felt dissatisfied in comparison, while accident victims were happy to simply get through the day without discomfort.

The third psychological factor underlying upward social comparisons are social norms. There are many social norms that influence our behavior in everyday life – we greet people with a hello, don't stare, donate to charity, recycle trash, and avoid using plastic bags. Many of these behaviors are voluntary, and the main reason we do them is that they are normative or expected by the society we live in. An important social norm that heightens upward social comparisons is the norm of competition. Most of us live in meritocratic societies that emphasize competition and reward the best performers in the workplace. Even in our personal lives, we are used to the idea of competition: we play the dating game, compete in the mate market, and encourage our children to top their classes. This competitive mindset encourages constant comparison with others as we size up others to get ahead in the human race. And who do we compare ourselves to? The hedonic treadmill highlights those who are doing better than ourselves, which, in turn, promotes upward social comparisons.

The fourth psychological factor that increases upward social comparison is evolution. Our minds and bodies today are the products of millions of years of evolution, during which the fittest survived to pass on their genes. Remember, only the fittest survived – not the somewhat fit or mostly fit, but the fittest. Since evolution rewarded those who were champions of their environments, our minds have evolved to focus on the top performers in our social milieu since they are the best examples to emulate for survival. And the more we use these high reference points, the stronger is our instinct for upward social comparisons.

The psychological reasons described above conspire to make upward social comparisons virtually irresistible. It is said that we are social animals. It would be more accurate to say that we are herd animals, searching for a group to follow and a leader to look up to. This hardwired tendency towards upward social comparisons can easily undermine our sense of well-being. For example, one research study investigated how happy employees in a firm were after getting a substantial raise at the end of the year (Card, Mas, Moretti, & Saez, 2012). Some employees in this study were simply told they were getting a raise. Others were told they were getting a raise and that their colleagues had also been given raises – with some colleagues getting bigger raises and others getting smaller raises. Not surprisingly, employees who were simply told that they had gotten a raise became much happier than before. In contrast, those who were told about their colleagues' raises were only marginally happier than before, even though they received the exact same amount of money. We can understand this paradox in terms of upward social comparison – when we hear about colleagues' raises, we automatically focus on colleagues who got a bigger raise rather than those who got a smaller raise than us, and this undermines happiness with our own raise.

So far, we have discussed upward social comparisons, that is, situations where we compare ourselves to others who are better off than us. However, upward social comparisons are not the only type of interpersonal comparison we can make. If we think more broadly, there are three possible types of comparisons: upward versus downward, social versus personal, and past versus present versus future. Let's illustrate these through the saying "the grass is always greener." Upward comparisons focus on grass that is greener than ours, while downward comparisons focus on grass that is less green than ours. Social comparisons focus attention on others' grass, while personal comparisons focus attention on our own grass. Past comparisons assess today's grass against the grass that grew last year; present comparisons are with the grass in our neighborhood today; and future comparisons refer to grass in the yards of tomorrow. It is important to keep all three types of comparisons in mind because they give us a broader perspective on the comparison process. They tell us that upward social comparisons are but one type of comparison and there are other ways we could compare aspects of our lives. As we will see shortly, these other types of comparisons might hold the key to taming upward social comparisons and improving our sense of well-being.

## What Can We Do?

The first step towards better comparisons is to understand that it is difficult to avoid upward social comparisons by force of will. As we saw earlier, upward social comparisons are driven by powerful psychological forces that are difficult to resist head-on. Furthermore, research has shown that trying not to think of something can have the opposite effect of bringing to mind the very thing we are trying to avoid (Wegner, 1994). For example, researchers have conducted studies where people were asked not to think about unusual objects such as "white bears." Ironically, it was found that giving such an instruction itself makes it more likely that white bears will come to mind. Similarly, if we consciously try not to think about other people's successes, this might actually make thoughts about others' successes more prominent in our minds. A better approach would be to supplement upward social comparisons with downward comparisons that we choose to make. For example, we could compare our current life situation with times in the past when we had less money, success, companionship, knowledge, or leisure. Similarly, we could compare our current lifestyle with that of others who are less fortunate than us. These downward comparisons will create feelings of gratefulness, which can act as an antidote to the envy generated by upward social comparisons. We can fight fire with water: envy with gratefulness.

One problem with downward comparisons is that gratitude does not seem to come naturally to people (Emmons & Crumpler, 2000; McCullough, Kilpatrick, Emmons, & Larson, 2001). While we automatically make upward comparisons, our minds resist making downward comparisons. One way to overcome our mental resistance to downward comparisons is to establish better habits of thought. Just as we can become practiced at things that initially seemed daunting – such as swimming, driving, or riding a bike – we can make downward comparisons second nature by diligently practicing gratitude at every opportunity. Research has shown that consistency is the father of habit (Bandura, 1977), and thus it is important to be consistently grateful for what we have even when it feels like a stretch. Over time, this will train our minds to automatically respond in a positive manner to the vicissitudes of life.

Two techniques are particularly useful for making a habit out of gratefulness. One is to write down, every night before going to bed, three things that went well during the day and why they went well. These events could be big or small, and the important thing is to write them down consistently every night without fail. Research has found that this exercise practiced for six months significantly increases happiness in life, even if the writing task is stopped after six months (Emmons & McCullough, 2003). A second method is to consciously think about a downward comparison every time we experience envy. To help us make these downward comparisons, we could prepare a "gratitude list" in advance and keep it on our phones or in our wallets to be consulted when required. As with any new habit, the earlier we start practicing downward comparisons the better, since early habits are easier to pick up and last longer than habits developed later in life.

Gratefulness is a gift that keeps on giving. Research on the halo effect has shown that gratefulness brings positive feelings to mind (Nisbett & Wilson, 1977). Other research shows that happy people are unaffected by the success or failure of others, whereas unhappy people are negatively affected by the superior performance of others (Lyubomirsky & Ross, 1999). Downward comparisons not only make us feel better about ourselves, they also increase our generosity towards others (Schlosser & Levy, 2016). Helping others, in turn, creates a virtuous cycle of stronger relationships and increased happiness in life.

Another step towards better comparisons is to take a more holistic view of cause and effect. When thinking about bad events in the past, people naturally focus on causes that were under their control (Roese & Olson, 1997). For example, when we think about an awkward date, poor job presentation, or burned dinner, we tend to think of things we did to cause these events without giving enough consideration to alternative causes such as others' behavior, bad luck, or poor advice. Of course, our actions can contribute to failures and we should learn from our mistakes. But it is useful to remember that many factors beyond our control also influence outcomes in life, and we don't naturally think of these factors when the chips are down. Making an effort to think of alternative causes will give us a more balanced view of our capabilities and increase our self-confidence in the face of life's disappointments. Ironically, even while we need to think less about our own influence on past events, we need to think more about how we can proactively influence future events. Focusing on what we can do to influence events in the future will increase our sense of control and thereby our motivation to work towards desirable outcomes.

Yet another useful step is to turn hot comparisons into cold comparisons. We have seen that upward social comparisons often create feelings of envy. "Hot" emotions such as envy dissipate slowly over time, leaving behind the "cold" factual comparison with others as a residue. For example, initial envy prompted by a colleague's promotion might slowly be replaced by a more rational comparison of job performance between yourself and your colleague. It is this rational or cold comparison with others, in the absence of emotions like envy, which helps us take the necessary steps to improve ourselves. Thus we should revisit our upward social comparisons after a day or two has passed and then write down a list of actions we need to take going forward. It is important to spell out our planned actions in writing rather than simply thinking about them. Research shows that writing down plans increases the likelihood of follow-through because the act of writing constitutes an initial commitment that our minds tend to stick to (Cialdini, Kallgren, & Reno, 1991; Shah & Kruglanski, 2003).

Another useful approach is to adopt a high-level construal in our thinking. Research shows that we can construe or view our environment in one of two ways – either with a high-level construal where we focus on ultimate outcomes, or with a low-level construal where we focus on intermediate processes (Trope & Liberman, 2003). For example, when planning a future vacation, we could adopt a high-level construal and think about ultimate outcomes such as relaxing on the beach or learning about a new culture. Alternatively, we could adopt a low-level construal where we focus on intermediate processes such as the flights we need to take or the budget we need to make. Research shows that people's construal level depends on three factors: temporal distance, physical distance, and social distance. Temporal distance refers to time – events in the near future or near past are viewed with a low-level construal, whereas events in the distant future or past are viewed with a high-level construal. Things that are physically close to us are viewed with a low-level construal, while those that are far away are viewed with a high-level construal. And people who are members of in-groups (i.e., social groups we already belong to) are viewed with a low-level construal while those belonging to out-groups are viewed with a high-level construal.

How can construal levels help us make better comparisons? Adopting a high-level construal keeps us focused on the big picture and thereby diminishes the significance of any one event. Thus, for example, a high-level construal might reduce the sting of upward comparison with a richer person by reminding us that money by itself does not buy happiness. We can adopt a high-level construal by working through the three drivers of construal level – we could take a longer-term view of decisions; we could distance ourselves physically from the decision context; and we could choose to think about people in out-groups rather than in-groups. For example, we could ask ourselves, "How much will this matter in three years?" or "What advice would I give someone else who was facing this situation?" The more broad and long-term is our thinking, the better social comparisons we will make.

Finally, we can benefit by adopting a satisficing rather than maximizing mindset. As discussed earlier, we can approach our decisions in two ways – with a satisficing mindset where we choose the first option that surpasses a threshold of acceptability, or with a maximizing mindset where we seek the best available option (Iyengar et al., 2006; Schwartz et al., 2002). Research has shown that satisficers are less likely to engage in upward social comparisons than maximizers (Schwartz et al., 2002). Participants in this study completed a questionnaire measuring the extent to which they were maximizers or satisficers and then reported the frequency of upward social comparisons in daily life. The researchers found that satisficers made fewer upward comparisons than maximizers for products as well as people in their lives. We too can reap this benefit by adopting a satisficing mindset, which will minimize the negative emotions generated by upward social comparisons.

# TOO LITTLE PRIVACY

The Internet never forgets. Everything we do online is recorded in credit card databases, Google archives, Facebook servers, computer cookies, and the electronic vaults of the NSA. If someone were to piece together the information we scatter online, they would know a lot about us – the brands we like, the movies we watch, our political views, and our sexual preferences. Data-mining firms like eXelate and Intellidyn do just this, collecting information about our online behavior and offering it to firms for marketing purposes. Facebook knows our age, gender, education, residence, travels, political views, and likes and dislikes for many products and services – information we have willingly provided them. Imagine if Facebook were to combine their records with commercially available data from credit card companies, credit rating agencies, and census databases: they would have more information about us than our closest friends and family. In fact, even a simple Google, Facebook, or LinkedIn search can turn up a lot of information we might consider private, such as our home address, employer, approximate salary, romantic relationships, and political views. The more time we spend online, the less privacy we have where privacy is "the right of individuals, groups, or institutions to determine for themselves when, how, and to what extent information is communicated to others" (Westin, 1967) – i.e., the right to be left alone.

Lack of privacy on the Internet is the latest chapter in a history of surveillance going back to ancient Egypt, where imperial records tracked births, deaths, immigration, taxation, agricultural production, and military service. The Book of Numbers in the Old Testament tells us that the nomadic people of Israel regularly conducted a census covering every member of the tribe. In the Middle Ages, the Domesday Book contained detailed property records of English land-holders and their dependents. In the twentieth century, Britain was the first country to create large-scale bureaucratic databases to facilitate conscription during the First World War. Today, the Chinese government uses databases to record not just the financial credit of citizens but also information about their social and political behavior.

Recent events have further increased the reach of the surveillance state. Since the financial crisis, governments have come under pressure to make the rich pay their fair share of taxes. As a result, authorities are now tracking incomes and expenditures more zealously than ever before. The United States requires foreign financial firms to report the transactions of all American clients, and more than 100 countries have signed up to the Common Reporting Standard, which requires them to regularly exchange information about foreign account holders. After 9/11 and other terrorist attacks, governments around the world have installed new surveillance tools to track their citizens in the name of security.

Our zone of privacy has shrunk not just online but also when we make phone calls or send text messages. These can be recorded by governments and Internet service providers, and layered with geolocation data from cell phone towers to create a detailed picture of our movements. Some of the devices we carry can be programmed to record data unobtrusively. Facebook has considered offering a mobile app that would turn on our cell phone microphones to identify songs or TV shows playing around us. The app would then automatically add a tag to our status showing, for example, that we are listening to the band Arcade Fire or watching *Game of Thrones*. Our privacy is also being eroded by the Internet of things, where household objects such as refrigerators, cars, and homes are connected to a virtual network. The IT analyst firm Gartner estimates that there will soon be 20 billion devices connected to the Internet of things (Gartner, 2015). Although these networks make products run more efficiently, they also increase the risk of hackers controlling our homes and accessing private information. Consider, for example, a car insurer who offers 20 percent off if you let them install a vehicle geo-tracker that monitors your driving skills. If you accept this offer, remember that the insurer will also know if you go to the liquor store three times a day, visit your doctor every Friday, and check into cheap motels on weekday afternoons. One day, this information could be used against you by hackers, governments, life insurance companies, or divorce lawyers.

The surveillance state is spreading from the online to the offline world. If you live in cities like London, Paris, New York, Dubai, Singapore, or Hong Kong, your public movements are constantly being recorded by CCTVs (closed-circuit televisions) on every street corner. The day is not far away when camera-mounted drones will patrol our skies to keep the peace. As the world's population becomes more urbanized, the unblinking eye of the surveillance camera will become our constant companion wherever we go. As Orwell predicted many years ago, Big Brother is now watching us.

## Costs of Too Little Privacy

Privacy is a natural human instinct because it offers a number of psychological benefits. We have a need for personal autonomy, which is served by maintaining a zone of privacy that separates us from others. We have a need for emotional release from the tensions of everyday life by entering a private area safe from prying eyes. We have a need for self-evaluation where we can retreat into our own space to reflect on life experiences, and privacy helps us set appropriate boundaries for different people and institutions. In addition, there are practical reasons for privacy, such as keeping potentially harmful medical, financial, or legal information from falling into the hands of those who might misuse it. WikiLeaks showed how governments intercept personal communications, and we often read about hackers breaking into financial, political, and business databases.

Given the importance of privacy, how concerned are people about their lack of online privacy? Early research on this topic indicated a relatively low level of privacy concern, but more recent studies indicate that such concerns are on the rise. An early study by Gross and Acquisti (2005) reported that Facebook users could easily be persuaded to hand over personal information such as their address and phone number, and relatively few Facebook users changed the permissive default privacy settings on their accounts. However, more recent studies show that Facebook users have become reluctant to share personal information, and many have proactively changed their privacy settings (Christofides, Muise, & Desmarais, 2009; Dey, Jelveh, & Ross, 2012; Fogel & Nehmad, 2009). A survey by the Pew Research Center reported that 81 percent of people do not feel secure about using social media to share private information, 68 percent feel that way about online chat, 57 percent about email, 46 percent about talking on cell phones, and 31 percent about talking on landlines. Not surprisingly, people who were aware of government surveillance programs were more likely to say that their communications were not secure. Interestingly, people seem to be equally distrustful of advertisers and government, with more than 70 percent of people expressing privacy concerns in both cases. Other common privacy concerns include misuse of personal information by malicious individuals for bullying, stalking, or character assassination and misuse by criminals for identity theft and financial fraud (Boyd & Ellison, 2007; Krasnova, Kolesnikova, & Guenther, 2009).

## The Privacy Gap

If people are becoming more concerned about privacy, we might expect them to act more carefully when they go online. Strangely enough, that's not what actually happens. One of the contradictions of the Internet is that people often express a concern about privacy when asked in surveys, but when it comes to actual online behavior, people act as if no one is watching them. Several studies have reported this "privacy gap" between expressed privacy concerns on one hand and observed online behavior on the other (Acquisti & Gross, 2006; Stutzman & Kramer-Duffield, 2010; Tufekci, 2008). For example, Acquisti and Gross (2006) found that the 16 percent of people who reported being "very worried" about the possibility that a stranger knew where they lived still revealed this information on their Facebook profile. More than 55 percent of respondents in the Pew study described earlier said they were willing to share information about themselves online in exchange for free samples. Sexting is common among teens, despite the ease with which supposedly private pictures and video can be posted online. People often download music and movies illegally; pornographic websites are among the most visited worldwide; and many politicians and public figures have been laid low by indiscreet tweets and Facebook posts. Even private correspondence and pictures are not safe – ask Jennifer Lawrence about stolen iCloud pictures or Hillary Clinton about hacked emails. In each of these cases, people discovered to their dismay that online behavior is never strictly private.

## Reasons for the Privacy Gap

Why is there a gap between expressed privacy concerns on one hand and actual online behavior on the other? One reason for the privacy gap is that different information is salient in our minds at different times. Survey questions about the Internet are often phrased broadly, such as "How concerned are you about your private information being accessed by others online?" When answering such general questions, people are likely to use their general knowledge about online privacy. Because there is frequent media coverage about violations of online privacy – the Snowden revelations or the Hillary Clinton email hack – people are likely to tell researchers in surveys that they too are concerned about the lack of online privacy. However, when people are browsing a particular website, factors other than privacy are more salient. For example, when we are on Facebook, we are busy browsing pictures, status updates, and personal messages from friends. Similarly, we focus on videos on YouTube, news on CNN, and products on Amazon. In all of these situations, we have more immediate objectives during browsing that take precedence in our minds over abstract concerns about privacy.

This mental bias in favor of the immediate and concrete is known as the availability bias (Tversky & Kahneman, 1973). The availability bias explains not only the privacy gap but also why people become overly fearful of terrorism after spectacular but one-off attacks such as 9/11; why drivers buy additional insurance after suffering a minor accident even though the probability of future accidents hasn't really changed; and why politicians prefer to use vivid stories and anecdotes in their speeches rather than statistical data. The concrete and vivid is more persuasive than the abstract and general. When we are browsing the Internet, the availability bias ensures that immediate and concrete objectives such as entertainment, social interaction, and information gathering loom larger in our minds than more abstract concerns about privacy. Another reason why the availability bias increases the privacy gap is that our own first-hand experiences are more salient to us than things we read or hear about from others. Since many of us have not personally suffered losses due to invasion of online privacy, the issue is not particularly salient when we go online. And when something is less salient at any given moment, the availability bias predicts that it will have a lesser effect on our online judgments and behavior.

Yet another reason for the privacy gap is our tendency to follow the behavior of others, which is known as the principle of social proof (Cialdini, 2004). Try this experiment yourself: Ask three of your friends to stand on a sidewalk and look up to the top of the nearest building. Very soon you will see that most passers-by are looking up as well. You may have seen signs in hotel bathrooms saying "more than 75 percent of our guests reuse towels." Research has shown that these signs are effective at increasing towel reuse because people tend to follow the behavior of previous guests (Goldstein, Cialdini, & Griskevicius, 2008). Similarly, electricity companies try to reduce energy consumption by informing customers that "most of your neighbors" have installed energy-efficient thermostats. Social proof operates on the Internet to normalize illegal downloading of movies or music – if most of my friends are doing it, I can do it too. Social proof has a stronger effect on our behavior when others doing the behavior are similar to ourselves. This is why illegal downloading is more common among younger people: they are surrounded by a large peer group of downloaders similar to them in terms of age, gender, and education.

The privacy gap is also driven by another psychological bias called hyperbolic discounting, which is a tendency to discount events in the distant future compared to the near future (Kirby & Herrnstein, 1995). Hyperbolic discounting explains why people often fail to save enough money for retirement, ignore the dangers of global warming, or indulge in chocolate cake when they are supposed to be on a diet. In each of these examples, the pleasure of the present looms larger than the price to be paid in the future. Online behaviors such as pirating movies or browsing extreme pornography provide immediate gratification, and hyperbolic discounting favors the pleasure of the moment over long-term concerns about privacy.

A fourth reason for the privacy gap is the self-positivity bias, which is our tendency to assume that we are special, and good things are more likely to happen to us than to other people (Menon, Block, & Ramanathan, 2002). I sometimes test the self-positivity bias in my classes by asking students on the first day of class to predict their expected grade at the end of the semester. I find that the majority of students say that they expect to get an A, even though the grading policy at my university – which students are well aware of – permits professors to award As to less than 10 percent of students. I don't tell students this, but the truth is most of them will not get the A they expect. Like the children of Lake Wobegon, most people consider themselves to be above average even though in fact this is mathematically impossible.

We can see the self-positivity bias at work in many other situations: entrepreneurs start businesses all the time hoping to create the next Google, even though failure is the norm for start-ups; high divorce rates don't deter people from getting married; and gamblers flock to casinos even though they know the odds are stacked heavily against them. People act as if fortune favors them even if the facts don't. The self-positivity bias on the Internet leads people to discount the likelihood of bad things happening to them such as stalking, trolling, identity theft, and financial fraud. Because of this discounting of personal risk, people's online behavior remains relatively unaffected by privacy concerns.

A fifth reason for the privacy gap is that we trust familiar brands. When we buy a new BMW, we trust that the car will deliver the promised horsepower and mileage, and we don't hire a mechanic to do an independent verification of the manufacturer's claims. When we buy Advil at the pharmacy, we trust that it contains the promised amount of ibuprofen without testing the tablet at a laboratory. Our online behavior is influenced by brand familiarity in a similar manner. When we share our personal pictures and information on Facebook, we trust that Facebook will not use our information in ways that can hurt us. The more familiar we are with brands such Facebook, Amazon, and PayPal, the less proof of privacy we will demand from them, and the more careless we will become about our online behavior.

A final reason for the privacy gap is our sense of anonymity on the Internet. The effect of anonymity on human behavior was examined in a study which monitored 27 houses in Seattle on the evening of Halloween (Diener, Fraser, Beaman, & Kelem, 1976). Inside each home was a table with two bowls: one filled with candy bars, the other with pennies and nickels. As children arrived in costume for trick-or-treat, they were asked by the host – who was actually a confederate in the study – to take only one candy and not to touch the money. The host then told the children that she had to get back to work in another room. In reality, the host was looking through a peephole to see how much candy or money the children would take.

The researchers were trying to understand whether perceived anonymity influences bad behaviors such as cheating and rule-breaking. To get to the bottom of this issue, researchers varied the anonymity of different groups of children by asking some kids their names and addresses while others were not asked any personal questions. The researchers found that children who felt anonymous because they had not been asked their names and addresses were much more likely to take forbidden candies and money – the rate of cheating was around 15 percent among children who gave their name and address, but more than 50 percent among those who were anonymous. The disinhibiting effect of anonymity is an important reason why otherwise law-abiding citizens take part in soccer riots and good students participate in hazing rituals at universities. People feel anonymous in crowds, and anonymity lowers the psychological barriers to bad behavior.

We usually browse the Internet by ourselves, and this solitude increases our sense of anonymity. Feeling anonymous, in turn, can increase negative online behaviors such as chatting with strangers, flaming, trolling, or expressing bigoted opinions. Indeed, research has shown that people are more willing to discuss controversial topics online when their identity is hidden (Chen & Berger, 2013). Of course, perceived anonymity is not always a bad thing. Research also shows that feeling anonymous can increase creativity because our thinking becomes less inhibited when we are not being watched and judged by others (Dahl & Moreau, 2002). An interesting implication of this finding is that Internet censorship in authoritarian countries could have an unexpected downside. Creativity flourishes when people feel they are not being watched, so countries that monitor their citizens' online behaviors may be sacrificing creativity and innovation for the short-term benefit of political control.

## What Can We Do?

Firms as well as individuals can take steps to close the privacy gap. One technique often used by firms is to publish a privacy policy on their websites. For example, websites such as Facebook, eBay, Expedia, and iTunes require users to read and assent to a privacy statement before using their services. The objective of these statements is to inform users about privacy risks so users can decide whether and how to interact with the website. However, an important problem with privacy statements is that they are drafted by lawyers and filled with dense language difficult to follow by regular folks. Research shows that complex messages are often ineffective because people either tune them out or misunderstand them (Chen & Chaiken, 1999; Petty & Cacioppo, 1986). So it is not surprising that few people actually read privacy statements before electronically agreeing to them (Martin & Murphy, 2017).

Another reason people sign privacy statements without reading them is the underweighting of rare events (Roth, Wänke, & Erev, 2016). For example, it has been found that people often don't buy insurance for rare events with catastrophic consequences such as airplane crashes and earthquakes (Erev & Roth, 2014). Similarly, people are likely to underweight rare but serious events such as their private online information being used maliciously. The more such negative outcomes are discounted, the more likely it is that people will thoughtlessly sign privacy statements without understanding the risks being described.

To address these shortcomings of privacy statements, firms sometimes publish shorter versions called privacy certifications. Two types of privacy certifications are commonly used. One is a seal granted by professional organizations such as the International Association of Privacy Professionals. These certifiers audit the privacy policies of client firms and issue a seal that can be electronically affixed to the client's website confirming that best privacy practices are being followed. Visitors to the website are also given a link to more information about the certification process. Although certifications are good because they are simple and visual, they also introduce a new problem. Just as people don't read long privacy statements, it is equally unlikely that people will take the trouble to check the bona fides of the firm issuing the certification. As a result, just about any certification – even from unknown or disreputable certifiers – might be accepted as valid, lulling users into thinking that privacy risk has been dealt with. And even when the certifying firm is dependable, there is a conflict of interest between certifiers and clients. Since certifiers are paid by clients, they might be tempted to issue a positive certification even when it is not warranted by the facts. There was a similar conflict of interest between credit rating agencies and banks before the financial crisis of 2008, and we know how that turned out. A more recent approach is to present privacy statements in visual form, such as graphic novels or short online videos. For example, iTunes has used a graphic novel called *Terms and Conditions* which informs users in an entertaining manner about the privacy implications of using their service. This playful take on privacy was able to shrink the iTunes privacy statement from 20,669 words to a shorter (and illustrated) 7,000 words.

Another type of privacy certification is endorsement by other users of the website, such as "trusted seller" ratings on eBay or Amazon. The higher the average "trusted seller" rating, the less the privacy risk should be for prospective customers. These crowd-sourced privacy certifications are useful because previous customers have no obvious reason to lie, and the rating itself is simple and easy to understand. However, this type of certification is useful only if many customers have submitted their ratings so that the sample size is large enough to permit reliable conclusions. Certifications are not useful when data is limited, such as when the seller is new to the market or when few customers have chosen to submit their ratings.

Firms can encourage safer online behavior by increasing the default security settings on browsers and apps. Browsers such as Firefox and Internet Explorer come with security settings that determine whether search histories are retained, cookies stored, pop-ups allowed, and passwords saved. These settings have default values chosen by the firm, which can subsequently be modified by the user. Interestingly, research has shown that people have a strong tendency to stick with defaults provided to them (Brown & Krishna, 2004). Consider the example of organ donations in different countries. Some countries such as the United Kingdom and Germany have an "opt-in" system where the default option is denial of permission to harvest organs after death, and where people have to proactively indicate willingness to donate their organs. In contrast, other countries such as France and Sweden have an "opt-out" system where people are assumed to have given permission for organ donation after death. Of course, people in these latter countries are free to change the default option by notifying authorities of their objection to organ harvesting after death.

It turns out that organ donation rates are very different in these two groups of countries, from a low of around 10 percent for opt-in countries to almost 100 percent for opt-out countries (Johnson & Goldstein, 2003). In other words, the decision to donate one's organs closely follows the default option: where the default option is to donate, almost everyone donates, but where the default option is not to donate, hardly anyone donates. Of course, one might wonder if these two groups of countries were different in other ways – culture, history, economics, or education – that could explain their different organ donation rates. Although possible, these alternative explanations are not very probable. The two groups of countries were mixed in terms of culture and history, so the effects of these factors should have washed out across the groups. Furthermore, both groups had similar economic and educational indicators, making it unlikely that these factors were driving differences in organ donation rates. This leaves default option as the most likely reason for the dramatic difference in donation rates among these two groups of countries. The power of default options suggests that firms should set default privacy settings at a high level since most users will end up keeping these settings and thereby enjoy greater online security. If firms don't take this action, governments should mandate high default privacy settings. Notably, such a mandate would not reduce people's freedom of action because users can always change their default setting at any time.

Another technique for influencing people towards safer online behavior is the privacy disclaimer. An example of privacy disclaimer is the cookie warning, which is now a required element of website and app design in Europe. This warning alerts users that the website is trying to install a cookie on their computer and asks the user to assent to the installation before continuing. Privacy disclaimers can also take the form of a "do not track" button, which allows users to use websites without leaving electronic traces of their visit. A problem with privacy disclaimers is that seeing these warnings regularly on websites and apps could habituate users and thus reduce their attention towards these disclaimers over time. This habituation problem is similar to health warnings on cigarette packages, which often become ineffective over time as people get used to them (White, Bariola, Faulkner, Coomber, & Wakefield, 2015).

So far, we have talked about steps that firms can take to reduce the privacy gap. We, as individuals, can also act more prudently online. First, we could increase the perceived presence of others around us when we go online. People sometimes browse the Internet in the presence of others in coffee shops and libraries. At other times, we browse the Internet alone at home or on the road. When others are visible to us, their presence will work through the availability bias to reduce perceptions of anonymity. And if we think we are less anonymous, we will be more circumspect in our browsing behavior. In contrast, when we surf the Internet alone, the availability bias magnifies our sense of anonymity, which encourages risky behavior. This implies that we should surf the Internet in the physical presence of others as much as possible. When browsing the Internet alone, we could increase the virtual presence of others by using pictures of people – family or friends – as screen savers on our device. Having their virtual eyes on us might reduce perceived anonymity and encourage safer browsing.

Smart devices in our homes – televisions, computers, phones, cars, and refrigerators – are programmed to collect data and automatically forward this to manufacturers. We can often disable this data collection in the settings menu of the device. It is important to remember that the more functions we use in a device, the more information is collected about our usage. Therefore, a good principle would be to deactivate features on products and services that we don't intend to use. We could also use data encryption tools such as

Tor or PGP that make it technically difficult for others to intercept our online communications. However, a problem with these tools is that they require a high degree of technical knowledge. Furthermore, they are not a permanent solution since encryption technologies quickly become obsolete and require an ongoing learning effort to stay ahead of the curve. A more fundamental solution would be to lower our expectations of privacy when we go online. If the Internet is a transparent medium by design, we could simply accept the fact that our privacy is limited in the virtual world and act accordingly.

# 6

# CONCLUSION

## Looking Back

The Internet will be our workshop and playground in the twenty-first century. What are the implications of this digital future? Will the Internet bring only benefits, or are there hidden dangers as well? We began by acknowledging the benefits of the Internet, such as increased choices, greater convenience, and greater ability to customize. We then saw that these benefits can backfire at times to create a minefield for users of the Internet. The preceding chapters mapped the minefield by highlighting five important costs of the Internet: too many temptations, too much information, too much customization, too many comparisons, and too little privacy. Understanding these costs can help us act more prudently; and if we do so, we will benefit from the enormous potential of the Internet for improving our lives.

A central idea in this book is that the five costs are a product of mental heuristics or shortcuts we are hardwired to use but which don't serve us well in an online environment. These heuristics can be understood by thinking of our mind as a clock. Just as clocks contain intricate movements with gears, flywheels, springs, and crystals that work in harmony to tell the correct time under normal circumstances, our minds too are complex organisms that usually make good – or at least good enough – judgments and decisions in most situations. But just as clocks can become inaccurate in hostile environments such as high heat or deep water, mental heuristics can malfunction in the face of excess information and endless temptations. We should also remember that the Internet has become omnipresent in less than a generation, which is less than a heartbeat in evolutionary time. This rapidity of change has not given our minds time to adjust and adapt to the challenges of the Internet. As a result, we often fall back on heuristics we are accustomed to using, not realizing these might lead to bad judgments and decisions in an online setting. Availability bias, confirmation bias, hyperbolic discounting, hedonic treadmill, self-positivity – these mental shortcuts help us in the real world but can hurt us in the online world. This book explains how misfiring of mental heuristics underlies the five costs, and how we can harness these same heuristics to become smarter users of the Internet.

If heuristics bias our judgments and decisions, we could ask: Why do people use heuristics in the first place? To answer this question, we need to revisit the traditional economic view of human beings and understand how this view has been enriched by psychology. A basic assumption of economic theory is that people make optimal choices – that is, consider all possible options, weigh the pros and cons of each option, and then choose the option with the best objective value. But this assumption about how we think is rarely, if ever, true. Consider a simple trip to the grocery store. Do we actively consider the thousands of products on the shelves, painstakingly assess the merits and demerits of each product, and only then fill our shopping baskets? We don't, because most choices in the real world have too many options, and we have too little time at our disposal and not enough mental capacity to optimize every decision. Even for important choices like accepting a job, buying a car, saving for retirement, or selecting a partner, we rarely optimize our decisions in the economic sense. Instead, we often let our emotions get the better of us, follow what others are doing, and use simple rules of thumb to make quick decisions. Rationality in the economic sense is often missing from group behavior as well – repeated booms and busts in the stock market, speculation and crashes in the housing market, and the rush to war after spectacular but one-off terrorist attacks show that societies as a whole can fail to make rational decisions even when the stakes are high.

If people are not perfectly rational as assumed by economists, what are they? The key contribution of psychology is to describe how people actually behave, rather than how they should behave in an artificial economic model of the world. Psychological analyses of behavior are based on concepts such as heuristics, emotions, and motivations – the cogs and wheels of our minds that drive decisions in daily life. The psychological approach sees the world as it is and tries to understand what makes real people tick – their hopes and fears, joys and tears, quirks and foibles. Instead of assuming that people are like Mr. Spock from the Star Trek movies or Hermione Granger from the Harry Potter books – characters who always analyze situations from a cool, logical perspective – psychology takes a more realistic view of people as short-sighted, short of breath, and short-handed in their decision-making. Psychology enriches economics by showing that choice optimization is really a special case of human behavior and that much of our behavior is actually driven by heuristics, emotional responses, and deep-seated needs.

## Looking Ahead

How will our relationship with the Internet evolve over time? What are the challenges and opportunities going forward? It is probably safe to say that the five costs of the Internet described in this book will increase over time. As the Internet expands globally, more people will go online and they will be able to do more things online. This will increase information, temptations, social comparisons, opportunities to customize, and threats to privacy. Of the five costs in this book, temptation, social comparison, and privacy are likely to be our biggest challenges in the future. Societies are already grappling with the twin dangers of rising inequality and income stagnation. A feeling that the system is rigged has increased popular support for radical political movements and inward-looking economic policies. This sense of alienation will be further stoked when the have-nots can go online to see how the other 1 percent lives: houses, yachts, cars, watches, gated communities, private schools, art collections, birthday celebrations, and vacation destinations. Besides material benefits, richer citizens also have other advantages such as greater social capital, opportunities for personal growth, and learned norms of professional behavior. The Internet will show all these advantages of the upper echelons – and disadvantages of the lower echelons – in great detail. This will increase temptations and social comparisons and could make the Internet a disruptive force in society.

As big data gets even bigger, our personal information will become less private. Google is already trying to connect the dots between what people look at online and what they purchase with their credit cards at advertisers' brick-and-mortar stores. This picture of customer activity can be further sharpened with information from Gmail, YouTube, Android, and census data. Everyone will be living on the network, whether they like it or not. Governments are beginning to use facial recognition technology to pinpoint the location of their citizens. Many jurisdictions in the United States now allow law enforcement to use scanned pictures from driving licenses for facial recognition searches. Whether we are chatting on Facebook or attending a protest in person, authorities now have the tools to know who we are and where we are.

Besides the five costs in this book, the Internet could have other negative effects as well, such as weakening of social ties and reduction of attention spans. Surfing the Internet is often a solitary activity, and even our interactions with others online are mediated by an electronic screen. Could this socially impoverished environment make it more difficult for future generations to learn skills such as interpreting body language, sustaining face-to-face conversation, and working together as a team? Lack of social skills, in turn, could accelerate a trend already visible: people now have fewer close friends, marry later if at all, and spend more of their time by themselves. The Internet could hasten this process of social atomization by making it easier to live an isolated life without strong ties to others. Perhaps religions and civic organizations will step into this breach and offer people an anchor of belonging in a rootless world. Perhaps nationalists and religious fanatics will use this opportunity to organize people into friends and enemies in conflict with each another.

Another danger of the Internet is that it will divide our attention into ever-thinner slices. We already carry around a clutch of electronic devices – smartwatch, fitness tracker, smartphone, tablet computer – that constantly demand our attention with updates, messages, calls, and games. Allocating attention in short bursts across micro-tasks could eventually degrade our ability to focus on larger tasks for extended periods of time. Activities that require sustained engagement might become more difficult – reading books, learning new hobbies, and writing letters could become rarer in the age of the Internet.

Many of our social interactions in the future will be with robots or virtual assistants programmed with artificial intelligence. In fact, we can already see voice-based assistants such as Apple's Siri and Amazon's Alexa being used in phones and homes. As these assistants become smarter and 3D technology allows us to interact with them in realistic virtual worlds, we might find artificial intelligence giving us the benefits of human company without its costs. Could virtual relationships replace relationships with real people? Should we treat our assistants as machines, friends, or servants? Will we start seeing human characteristics in our virtual helpers? Will our license to treat virtual helpers as we please make us less civil to fellow human beings? Our challenge will be to find an optimal balance between human and machine interaction that maintains our repertoire of social skills and identity as human beings.

Yet another challenge is the blurring of entertainment and advertising on the Internet. Brands are increasingly abandoning traditional video and banner advertising, which consumers can block with software or ignore by switching to other screens. To reach consumers in this fickle environment, brands are instead offering free information or entertainment and embedding their message within free content. For example, a brand of athletic shoe might sponsor a running website or live-stream a sports event where the brand is prominently featured. This type of advertising is more insidious because our natural defenses against persuasion are lower when we are not expecting to be sold to. In the 1950s and 1960s, it was widely believed that subliminal messages embedded in advertising could subtly influence people into buying things. Subsequent research showed that subliminal advertising is more myth than reality, and it is very difficult to change people's behavior using hidden messages in ads. Although subliminal advertising did not live up to its hype, today's Internet could turn out to be the real hidden persuader working through sponsored entertainment, fake news, and echo chambers of like-minded people.

Although the costs of the Internet are likely to increase with time, we also have the power to minimize these costs by taking appropriate action. For example, we saw that deciding not to choose is as important as deciding what to choose; setting up structural barriers to temptation can reduce overspending; and comparisons with others on social media should be cold rather than hot. Another useful step might be to take an occasional "Internet detox." Just as it is good for our bodies to go on a nutritional fast from time to time, it may be good to take a break from the Internet to refresh our minds.

For example, we could book vacation destinations without Internet or cellphone coverage and lock up our electronic devices in the office before we leave. An Internet detox would reduce exposure to the five costs and give us more opportunity to interact with people in the real world. Of course, starting and sticking to an Internet detox will require self-control. We could increase our self-control by making non-refundable deposits on vacation destinations without Internet access and installing software that locks our devices out of the Internet for specified periods of time. Policymakers can help by mandating Internet time-outs, an example of which are European laws restricting employers from emailing employees after working hours.

Educational initiatives can increase awareness of the psychological costs of the Internet. One approach currently being tested relates to online privacy. University-level accreditation in computer science now often requires knowledge of the social and ethical implications of computing. This approach could be extended to other costs of the Internet, using educational materials developed for use in schools and universities. Similar to financial literary, Internet literacy – technical and psychological – could become a basic life skill imparted to citizens by the educational system.

Although this book is about the dark side of the Internet, I would like to end on a more positive note. Our social circle in the past was limited by history and geography – the history of people we knew and the geography of where we happened to live. The Internet has freed us from these constraints and opened up a new world of opportunities. We can learn from the best teachers for free; get business ideas from around the world; crowdsource funding from people rather than banks; and find love, friendships, and hookups on demand. Social media can foster a culture of openness and trust by encouraging people to share intimate details of their lives. The Internet can make our economy more sustainable by encouraging sharing rather than buying products and services. Perhaps over time, our current economy based on individual ownership and wasteful consumption will evolve into an online sharing economy based on minimum usage and maximum conservation. This bright digital future can be ours if we use the Internet in a thoughtful way, keeping in mind the five costs of living online.

# ACKNOWLEDGMENTS

This book lists my name as the author but should really be credited to the many people who helped me on this journey. I have to start with my acquisitions editor, Jennifer DiDomenico, who encouraged me to embark on this project and nurtured it to completion. This book is based on research, and I am grateful to all my research collaborators, especially Wayne Hoyer, Andrew Gershoff, Raj Raghunathan, and many others. I am truly lucky to have such knowledgeable and generous people in my life – friends I can turn to for ideas, advice, and help. I am in debt to the reviewers who saw potential in early versions of this book and offered many suggestions for improvement. A large part of this book was written during a sabbatical leave granted by McGill University, for which I am thankful. I would also like to acknowledge financial support for my research from the Social Sciences and Humanities Research Council of Canada. Finally, whatever I have accomplished is because of the unconditional love and support of my family – my parents Ena and Ashim, my wife Vladimira, daughter Tara, and sisters Pia and Panchali. Thank you for everything.

# REFERENCES

Acquisti, A., & Gross, R. (2006). Imagined communities: Awareness, information sharing, and privacy on the Facebook. International Workshop on Privacy Enhancing Technologies, PET, 36–58.

Acquisti, A., & Varian, H.R. (2005). Conditioning prices on purchase history. *Marketing Science, 24*(3), 367–81. https://doi.org/10.1287/mksc.1040.0103

Ainslie, G. (1992). *Picoeconomics: The strategic interaction of successive motivational states within the person.* New York, NY: Cambridge University Press.

Ajzen, I. (2002). Perceived behavioral control, self-efficacy, locus of control, and the theory of planned behavior. *Journal of Applied Social Psychology, 32*(4), 665–83. https://doi.org/10.1111/j.1559-1816.2002.tb00236.x

Anderson, C. (2006). *The long tail.* New York, NY: Hyperion.

Atalay, S., & Meloy, M.G. (2011). Retail therapy: A strategic effort to improve mood. *Psychology and Marketing, 28*(6), 638–59. https://doi.org/10.1002/mar.20404

Auschaitrakul, S., & Mukherjee, A. (2014). *Social network use: Social comparisons and their emotional consequences.* Miami, FL: Society for Consumer Psychology.

Auschaitrakul, S., & Mukherjee, A. (2017). Online display advertising: The influence of website type on advertising effectiveness. *Psychology and Marketing, 34*(4), 463–80. https://doi.org/10.1002/mar.21000

Bandura, A. (1977). Self-efficacy: Toward a unifying theory of behavioral change. *Psychological Review, 84*(2), 191–215. https://doi.org/10.1037/0033-295X.84.2.191

Barasch, A., & Berger, J. (2014). Broadcasting and narrowcasting: How audience size affects what people share. *Journal of Marketing Research, 51*(3), 286–99. https://doi.org/10.1509/jmr.13.0238

Baumeister, R.F. (2002). Yielding to temptation: Self-control failure, impulsive purchasing, and consumer behavior. *Journal of Consumer Research, 28*(4), 670–6. https://doi.org/10.1086/338209

Berger, J., & Iyengar, R. (2013). Communication channels and word of mouth: How the medium shapes the message. *Journal of Consumer Research, 40*(3), 567–79. https://doi.org/10.1086/671345

Bettman, J.R., Luce, M.F., & Payne, J.W. (1998). Constructive consumer choice processes. *Journal of Consumer Research, 25*(3), 187–217. https://doi.org/10.1086/209535

Boyd, D.M., & Ellison, N.B. (2007). Social network sites: Definition, history, and scholarship. *Journal of Computer-Mediated Communication, 13*(1), 210–30. https://doi.org/10.1111/j.1083-6101.2007.00393.x

Brickman, P., Coates, D., & Janoff-Bulman, R. (1978). Lottery winners and accident victims: Is happiness relative? *Journal of Personality and Social Psychology, 36*(8), 917–27. https://doi.org/10.1037/0022-3514.36.8.917

Brown, C.L., & Krishna, A. (2004). The skeptical shopper: A metacognitive account for the effects of default options on choice. *Journal of Consumer Research, 31*(3), 529–39. https://doi.org/10.1086/425087

Buechel, E.C., & Janiszewski, C. (2014). Lot of work or a work of art: How the structure of a customized assembly task determines the utility derived from assembly effort. *Journal of Consumer Research, 40*(5), 960–72.

Campbell, J.D., Trapnell, P.D., Heine, S.J., Katz, I.M., Lavallee, L.F., & Lehman, D.R. (1996). Self-concept clarity: Measurement, personality correlates, and cultural boundaries. *Journal of Personality and Social Psychology, 70*(1), 141–56. https://doi.org/10.1037/0022-3514.70.1.141

Card, D., Mas, A., Moretti, E., & Saez, E. (2012). Inequality at work: The effect of peer salaries on job satisfaction. *American Economic Review, 102*(6), 2981–3003. https://doi.org/10.1257/aer.102.6.2981

Carmon, Z., Wertenbroch, K., & Zeelenberg, M. (2003). Option attachment: When deliberating makes choosing feel like losing. *Journal of Consumer Research, 30*(1), 15–29. https://doi.org/10.1086/374701

Chan, H., & Cui, S. (2011). The contrasting effects of negative word of mouth in the post-consumption stage. *Journal of Consumer Psychology, 21*(3), 324–37. https://doi.org/10.1016/j.jcps.2010.11.005

Chen, S., & Chaiken, S. (1999). The heuristic-systematic model in its broader context. In S. Chaiken & Y. Trope (Eds.), *Dual-process theories in social psychology* (pp. 73–96). New York, NY: Guilford Press.

Chen, Z., & Berger, J. (2013). When, why, and how controversy causes conversation. *Journal of Consumer Research, 40*(3), 580–93. https://doi.org/10.1086/671465

Christofides, E., Muise, A., & Desmarais, S. (2009). Information disclosure and control on Facebook: Are they two sides of the same coin or two different processes? *Cyberpsychology & Behavior, 12*(3), 341–5. https://doi. org/10.1089/cpb.2008.0226

Chung, T.S., Wedel, M., & Rust, R.T. (2016). Adaptive personalization using social networks. *Journal of the Academy of Marketing Science, 44*(1), 66–87. https://doi.org/10.1007/s11747-015-0441-x

Cialdini, R. (2001, October). Harnessing the science of persuasion. *Harvard Business Review*, 72–9.

Cialdini, R.B. (2004). The science of persuasion. *Scientific American Mind, 14*(1), 70–7.

Cialdini, R.B., Kallgren, C.A., & Reno, R.R. (1991). A focus theory of normative conduct: A theoretical refinement and reevaluation of the role of norms in human behavior. *Advances in Experimental Social Psychology, 24*, 201–34. https://doi.org/10.1016/S0065-2601(08)60330-5

Confer, J.C., Perilloux, C., & Buss, D. (2010). More than just a pretty face: Men's priority shifts towards bodily attractiveness in short-term versus long-term mating contexts. *Evolution and Human Behavior, 31*(5), 348–53. https://doi.org/10.1016/j.evolhumbehav.2010.04.002

Csikszentmihalyi, M. (1996). *Flow and the psychology of discovery and invention.* New York, NY: HarperCollins.

Dahl, D.W., & Moreau, P. (2002). The influence and value of analogical thinking during new product ideation. *Journal of Marketing Research, 39*(1), 47–60. https://doi.org/10.1509/jmkr.39.1.47.18930

Dahl, D.W., & Moreau, C.P. (2007). Thinking inside the box: Why consumers enjoy constrained creative experiences. *Journal of Marketing Research, 44*(3), 357–69. https://doi.org/10.1509/jmkr.44.3.357

Dellaert, B.G.C., & Häubl, G. (2012). Searching in choice mode: Consumer decision processes in product search with recommendations. *Journal of Marketing Research, 49*(2), 277–88. https://doi.org/10.1509/jmr.09.0481

Dey, R., Jelveh, Z., & Ross, K. (2012, March). Facebook users have become much more private: A large-scale study. In *Pervasive Computing and Communications Workshops (PERCOM Workshops)*, IEEE, 346–52. https://doi. org/10.1109/PerComW.2012.6197508

Diener, E., Fraser, S.C., Beaman, A.L., & Kelem, R.T. (1976). Effects of deindividuation variables on stealing among Halloween trick-or-treaters. *Journal of Personality and Social Psychology, 33*(2), 178–83. https://doi. org/10.1037/0022-3514.33.2.178

Diener, E., Lucas, R.E., & Scollon, C. (2006). Beyond the hedonic treadmill: Revising the adaptation theory of well-being. *American Psychologist, 61*(4), 305–14. https://doi.org/10.1037/0003-066X.61.4.305

Dimoka, A. (2010). What does the brain tell us about trust and distrust? Evidence from a functional neuroimaging study. *Management Information Systems Quarterly, 34*(2), 373–96.

Ding, M., Grewal, R., & Liechty, J. (2005). Incentive-aligned conjoint analysis. *Journal of Marketing Research, 42*(1), 67–82. https://doi.org/10.1509/jmkr.42.1.67.56890

Emmons, R.A., & Crumpler, C.A. (2000). Gratitude as a human strength: Appraising the evidence. *Journal of Social and Clinical Psychology, 19*(1), 56–69. https://doi.org/10.1521/jscp.2000.19.1.56

Emmons, R.A., & McCullough, M.E. (2003). Counting blessings versus burdens: An experimental investigation of gratitude and subjective well-being in daily life. *Journal of Personality and Social Psychology, 84*(2), 377–89. https://doi.org/10.1037/0022-3514.84.2.377

Epstein, R., & Robertson, R.E. (2015). The search engine manipulation effect (SEME) and its possible impact on the outcomes of elections. *Proceedings of the National Academy of Sciences of the United States of America, 112*(33), E4512–E4521. https://doi.org/10.1073/pnas.1419828112

Erev, I., & Roth, A.E. (2014). Maximization, learning, and economic behavior. *Proceedings of the National Academy of Sciences of the United States of America, 111*(Suppl. 3), 10818–25. https://doi.org/10.1073/pnas.1402846111

Faber, R., & Vohs, K. (2004). To buy or not to buy: Self-control and self-regulatory failure in self-control. In R.F. Baumeister & K.D. Vohs (Eds.), *Handbook of self-regulation: Research, theory, and applications* (pp. 509–24). New York, NY: Guilford Press.

Ferguson, C.J. (2010). Blazing angels or resident evil? *Journal of General Psychology, 14*(2), 68–81.

Festinger, L. (1954). A theory of social comparison processes. *Human Relations, 7*(2), 117–40. https://doi.org/10.1177/001872675400700202

Fogel, J., & Nehmad, E. (2009). Internet social network communities: Risk taking, trust, and privacy concerns. *Computers in Human Behavior, 25*(1), 153–60. https://doi.org/10.1016/j.chb.2008.08.006

Frederick, S., & Loewenstein, G. (1999). Hedonic adaptation. In D. Kahneman, E. Diener, & N. Schwarz (Eds.), *Well-being: Foundations of hedonic psychology* (pp. 302–29). New York, NY: Russell Sage Foundation.

Freeman, K., Spenner, P., & Bird, A. (2012, May 23). Three myths about what customers want. *Harvard Business Review*.

Fuchs, C., Prandelli, E., Schreier, M., & Dahl, D.W. (2013). All that is users might not be gold: How labeling products as user designed backfires in the context of luxury fashion brands. *Journal of Marketing, 77*(5), 75–91. https://doi.org/10.1509/jm.11.0330

Galinsky, A.D., Ku, G., & Wang, C.S. (2005). Perspective-taking and self-other overlap: Fostering social bonds and facilitating social coordination. *Group Processes & Intergroup Relations, 8*(2), 109–24. https://doi.org/10.1177/1368430205051060

Gartner. (2015, November 10). *Gartner says 6.4 billion connected things will be in use in 2016, up 30 percent from 2015* [Press release].

Gershman, B. (2014). The two sides to envy. *Journal of Economic Growth, 19*(4), 407–38. https://doi.org/10.1007/s10887-014-9106-8

Gershoff, A.D., Mukherjee, A., & Mukhopadhyay, A. (2007). Few ways to love, but many ways to hate: Attribute ambiguity and the positivity effect in agent evaluation. *Journal of Consumer Research, 33*(4), 499–505. https://doi.org/10.1086/510223

Goldstein, N.J., Cialdini, R.B., & Griskevicius, V. (2008). A room with a viewpoint: Using social norms to motivate environmental conservation in hotels. *Journal of Consumer Research, 35*(3), 472–82. https://doi.org/10.1086/586910

Goodman, J., & Irmak, C. (2013). Having versus consuming: Failure to estimate usage frequency makes consumer prefer multifeature products. *Journal of Marketing Research, 50*(1), 44–54. https://doi.org/10.1509/jmr.10.0396

Griffiths, M. (2001). Sex on the Internet: Observations and implications for Internet sex addiction. *Journal of Sex Research, 38*(4), 333–42. https://doi.org/10.1080/00224490109552104

Gross, R., & Acquisti, A. (2005). Information revelation and privacy in online social networks. In *Proceedings of the 2005 ACM workshop on privacy in the electronic society*, 71–80. https://doi.org/10.1145/1102199.1102214

Hansen, T., Mukherjee, A., & Uth Thomsen, T. (2011). Anxiety and search during food choice: The moderating role of attitude towards nutritional claims. *Journal of Consumer Marketing, 28*(3), 178–86. https://doi.org/10.1108/07363761111127608

Hauser, J.R., Urban, G.R., Liberali, C., & Braun, M. (2009). Website morphing. *Marketing Science, 28*(2), 202–23.

Hoch, S.J., & Deighton, J. (1989). Managing what consumers learn from experience. *Journal of Marketing, 53*(2), 1–20. https://doi.org/10.2307/1251410

Hoeffler, S. (2003). Measuring preferences for really new products. *Journal of Marketing Research, 40*(4), 406–20. https://doi.org/10.1509/jmkr.40.4.406.19394

Hoyer, W.D., & Brown, S.P. (1990). Effects of brand awareness on choice for a common, repeat-purchase product. *Journal of Consumer Research, 17*(2), 141–8. https://doi.org/10.1086/208544

Iyengar, S. (2011). *The art of choosing*. New York, NY: Twelve.

Iyengar, S.S., & Lepper, M.R. (2000). When choice is demotivating: Can one desire too much of a good thing? *Journal of Personality and Social Psychology, 79*(6), 995–1006. https://doi.org/10.1037/0022-3514.79.6.995

Iyengar, S.S., Wells, R.E., & Schwartz, B. (2006). Doing better but feeling worse: Looking for the "best" job undermines satisfaction. *Psychological Science, 17*(2), 143–50. https://doi.org/10.1111/j.1467-9280.2006.01677.x

Jasny, L., Waggle, J., & Fisher, D. (2015). An empirical examination of echo chambers in US climate policy networks. *Nature Climate Change, 5,* 782–6. https://doi.org/10.1038/nclimate2666

Johnson, E.J., & Goldstein, D. (2003). Do defaults save lives? *Science, 302*(5649), 1338–9. https://doi.org/10.1126/science.1091721

Kahneman, D., Knetsch, J.L., & Thaler, R.H. (1990). Experimental tests of the endowment effect and the Coase theorem. *Journal of Political Economy, 98*(6), 1325–48. https://doi.org/10.1086/261737

Kannan, P.K., Pope, B.K., & Jain, S. (2009). Pricing digital content product lines: A model and application for the National Academies Press. *Marketing Science, 28*(4), 620–36. https://doi.org/10.1287/mksc.1080.0481

Khan, U., Dhar, R., & Wertenbroch, K. (2005). A behavioral decision theory perspective on hedonic and utilitarian choice. In S. Ratneshwar & D. Mick (Eds.), *Inside consumption: Consumer motives, goals, and desires* (pp. 144–64). London, UK: Routledge.

Kirby, K.N., & Herrnstein, R.J. (1995, March). Preference reversals due to myopic discounting of delayed reward. *Psychological Science, 6*(2), 83–9. https://doi.org/10.1111/j.1467-9280.1995.tb00311.x

Krasnova, H., Kolesnikova, E., & Guenther, O. (2009). It won't happen to me! Self-disclosure in online social networks. In *Proceedings of the Fifteenth Americas Conference on Information Systems, 343,* 1–10.

Loewenstein, G. (1996). Out of control: Visceral influences on behavior. *Organizational Behavior and Human Decision Processes, 65*(3), 272–92. https://doi.org/10.1006/obhd.1996.0028

Loewenstein, G. (2005). Hot-cold empathy gaps and medical decision making. *Health Psychology, 24*(Suppl. 4), S49–S56. https://doi.org/10.1037/0278-6133.24.4.S49

Lyubomirsky, S., & Ross, L. (1999). Changes in attractiveness of elected, rejected, and precluded alternatives: A comparison of happy and unhappy individuals. *Journal of Personality and Social Psychology, 76*(6), 988–1007. https://doi.org/10.1037/0022-3514.76.6.988

Martin, K., & Murphy, P. (2017). The role of data privacy in marketing. *Journal of the Academy of Marketing Science, 45*(2), 135–55. https://doi.org/10.1007/s11747-016-0495-4

McCullough, M.E., Kilpatrick, S.D., Emmons, R.A., & Larson, D.B. (2001). Is gratitude a moral affect? *Psychological Bulletin, 127*(2), 249–66. https://doi.org/10.1037/0033-2909.127.2.249

McFerran, B., Dahl, D.W., Fitzsimons, G.J., & Morales, A.C. (2010). Might an overweight waitress make you eat more? How the body type of others is

sufficient to alter our food consumption. *Journal of Consumer Psychology,*
*20*(2), 146–51. https://doi.org/10.1016/j.jcps.2010.03.006

McGraw, A.P., Schwartz, J.A., & Tetlock, P.E. (2012). From the commercial to
the communal: Reframing taboo trade-offs in religious and pharmaceutical
marketing. *Journal of Consumer Research, 39*(1), 157–73. https://doi.
org/10.1086/662070

Menon, G., Block, L., & Ramanathan, S. (2002). We're at as much risk as we are
led to believe: Effects of message cues on judgments of health risk. *Journal of*
*Consumer Research, 28*(4), 533–49. https://doi.org/10.1086/338203

Mischel, W., Ebbesen, E.B., & Raskoff Zeiss, A. (1972). Cognitive and
attentional mechanisms in delay of gratification. *Journal of Personality and*
*Social Psychology, 21*(2), 204–18. https://doi.org/10.1037/h0032198

Mori, M., MacDorman, K.F., & Kageki, N. (2012). The uncanny valley. *IEEE*
*Robotics & Automation Magazine, 19*(2), 98–100. https://doi.org/10.1109/
MRA.2012.2192811

Mukherjee, A. (2017). Health shortcuts and food choice. Unpublished
manuscript.

Mukherjee, A., & Hoyer, W.D. (2001). The effect of novel attributes on
product evaluation. *Journal of Consumer Research, 28*(3), 462–72. https://doi.
org/10.1086/323733

Mukhopadhyay, A., & Johar, G.V. (2005). Where there is a will, is there a way?
Effects of lay theories of self-control on setting and keeping resolutions.
*Journal of Consumer Research, 31*(4), 779–86. https://doi.org/10.1086/426611

Muraven, M., & Baumeister, R.F. (2000). Self-regulation and depletion of
limited resources: Does self-control resemble a muscle? *Psychological*
*Bulletin, 126*(2), 247–59. https://doi.org/10.1037/0033-2909.126.2.247

Mussweiler, T., Rüter, K., & Epstude, K. (2004). The ups and downs of social
comparison: Mechanisms of assimilation and contrast. *Journal of Personality*
*and Social Psychology, 87*(6), 832–44. https://doi.org/10.1037/0022-
3514.87.6.832

Nielsen. (2015). *Global trust in advertising.* https://www.nielsen.com/content/
dam/nielsenglobal/apac/docs/reports/2015/nielsen-global-trust-in-
advertising-report-september-2015.pdf

Nisbett, R.E., & Wilson, T.D. (1977). The halo effect: Evidence for unconscious
alteration of judgments. *Journal of Personality and Social Psychology, 35*(4),
250–6. https://doi.org/10.1037/0022-3514.35.4.250

Nowlis, S.M., Khan, B.E., & Dhar, R. (2002). Coping with ambivalence: The
effect of removing a neutral option on consumer attitude and preference
judgments. *Journal of Consumer Research, 29*(3), 319–34. https://doi.
org/10.1086/344431

Peck, J., & Shu, S.B. (2009). The effect of mere touch on perceived ownership.
*Journal of Consumer Research, 36*(3), 434–47. https://doi.org/10.1086/598614

Petty, R.E., & Cacioppo, J.T. (1986). *Communication and persuasion: Central and peripheral routes to attitude change*. New York, NY: Springer. https://doi.org/10.1007/978-1-4612-4964-1

Pieters, R., & Warlop, L. (1999). Visual attention during brand choice: The impact of time pressure and task motivation. *International Journal of Research in Marketing, 16*(1), 1–16. https://doi.org/10.1016/S0167-8116(98)00022-6

Print my ride. (2016, June 23). *Economist*.

Redelmeier, D.A., & Shafir, E. (1995). Medical decision making in situations that offer multiple alternatives. *Journal of the American Medical Association, 273*(4), 302–5. https://doi.org/10.1001/jama.1995.03520280048038

Roese, N., & Olson, J. (1997). Counterfactual thinking: The intersection of affect and function. *Advances in Experimental Social Psychology, 29*, 1–59. https://doi.org/10.1016/S0065-2601(08)60015-5

Roth, Y., Wänke, M., & Erev, I. (2016). Click or skip: The role of experience in easy-click checking decisions. *Journal of Consumer Research, 43*(4), 583–97. https://doi.org/10.1093/jcr/ucw053

Schlosser, A.E., & Levy, E. (2016). Helping others or oneself: How direction of comparison affects prosocial behavior. *Journal of Consumer Psychology, 26*(4), 461–73. https://doi.org/10.1016/j.jcps.2016.02.002

Schwartz, B., Ward, A., Monterosso, J., Lyubomirsky, S., White, K., & Lehman, D.R. (2002). Maximizing versus satisficing: Happiness is a matter of choice. *Journal of Personality and Social Psychology, 83*(5), 1178–97. https://doi.org/10.1037/0022-3514.83.5.1178

Sela, A., Berger, J., & Liu, W. (2009). Variety, vice, and virtue: How assortment size influences option choice. *Journal of Consumer Research, 35*(6), 941–51. https://doi.org/10.1086/593692

Shafir, E., Simonson, I., & Tversky, A. (1993). Reason-based choice. *Cognition, 49*(1), 11–36. https://doi.org/10.1016/0010-0277(93)90034-S

Shah, J.Y., & Kruglanski, A.W. (2003). When opportunity knocks: Bottom-up priming of goals by means and its effects on self-regulation. *Journal of Personality and Social Psychology, 84*(6), 1109–22. https://doi.org/10.1037/0022-3514.84.6.1109

Shiv, B., Carmon, Z., & Ariely, D. (2005). Placebo effects of marketing actions: Consumers may get what they pay for. *Journal of Marketing Research, 42*(4), 383–93. https://doi.org/10.1509/jmkr.2005.42.4.383

Sparrow, B., & Chatman, L. (2013). Social cognition in the Internet age: Same as it ever was? *Psychological Inquiry: An International Journal for the Advancement of Psychological Theory, 24*(4), 273–92. https://doi.org/10.1080/1047840X.2013.827079

Sparrow, B., Liu, J., & Wegner, D.M. (2011). Google effects on memory: Cognitive consequences of having information at our fingertips. *Science, 333*(6043), 776–8. https://doi.org/10.1126/science.1207745

Stroebe, W., Mensink, W., Aarts, H., Schut, H., & Kruglanski, A.W. (2008). Why dieters fail: Testing the goal conflict model of eating. *Journal of Experimental Social Psychology, 44*(1), 26–36. https://doi.org/10.1016/j.jesp.2007.01.005

Stutzman, F., & Kramer-Duffield, J. (2010). Friends only: Examining a privacy-enhancing behavior in Facebook. In *Proceedings of the SIGCHI Conference on Human Factors in Computing Systems*, 1553–62. https://doi.org/10.1145/1753326.1753559

Summerville, A., & Roese, N.J. (2008). Self-report measures of individual differences in regulatory focus: A cautionary note. *Journal of Research in Personality, 42*(1), 247–54. https://doi.org/10.1016/j.jrp.2007.05.005

Szymanski, D.M., & Henard, D.H. (2001). Customer satisfaction: A meta-analysis of the empirical evidence. *Journal of the Academy of Marketing Science, 29*(1), 16–35. https://doi.org/10.1177/0092070301291002

Taylor, S.E., & Brown, J.D. (1988). Illusion and well-being: A social psychological perspective on mental health. *Psychological Bulletin, 103*(2), 193–210. https://doi.org/10.1037/0033-2909.103.2.193

Trope, Y., & Liberman, N. (2003). Temporal construal. *Psychological Review, 110*(3), 403–21. https://doi.org/10.1037/0033-295X.110.3.403

Trotzke, P., Starcke, K., Müller, A., & Brand, M. (2015). Pathological buying online as a specific form of internet addiction: A model-based experimental investigation. *PLoS One, 10*(10), e0140296. https://doi.org/10.1371/journal.pone.0140296

Tufekci, Z. (2008). Grooming, gossip, Facebook and Myspace. *Information Communication and Society, 11*(4), 544–64. https://doi.org/10.1080/13691180801999050

Tversky, A., & Kahneman, D. (1973). Availability: A heuristic for judging frequency and probability. *Cognitive Psychology, 5*(2), 207–32. https://doi.org/10.1016/0010-0285(73)90033-9

Tversky, A., & Kahneman, D. (1983). Extensional versus intuitive reasoning: The conjunction fallacy in probability judgment. *Psychological Review, 90*(4), 293–315. https://doi.org/10.1037/0033-295X.90.4.293

The tyranny of choice. (2010, December 16). *Economist.*

Van Boven, L., & Gilovich, T. (2003). To do or to have: That is the question. *Journal of Personality and Social Psychology, 85*(6), 1193–202. https://doi.org/10.1037/0022-3514.85.6.1193

van de Ven, N., Zeelenberg, M., & Pieters, R. (2009). Leveling up and down: The experiences of benign and malicious envy. *Emotion, 9*(3), 419–29. https://doi.org/10.1037/a0015669

Wegner, D.M. (1994). Ironic processes of mental control. *Psychological Review, 101*(1), 34–52. https://doi.org/10.1037/0033-295X.101.1.34

Westin, A. (1967). *Privacy and freedom.* New York, NY: Atheneum.

White, V., Bariola, E., Faulkner, A., Coomber, K., & Wakefield, M. (2015). Graphic health warnings on cigarette packs: How long before the effects on adolescents wear out? *Nicotine & Tobacco Research, 17*(7), 776–83. https://doi.org/10.1093/ntr/ntu184

Wilcox, K., & Stephen, A.T. (2013). Are close friends the enemy? Online social networks, self-esteem, and self-control. *Journal of Consumer Research, 40*(1), 90–103. https://doi.org/10.1086/668794

Wood, J.V. (1989). Theory and research concerning social comparisons of personal attributes. *Psychological Bulletin, 106*(2), 231–48. https://doi.org/10.1037/0033-2909.106.2.231

Wood, W., & Neal, D.T. (2007). A new look at habits and the habit-goal interface. *Psychological Review, 114*(4), 843–63. https://doi.org/10.1037/0033-295X.114.4.843

Wyer, R.S., Jr., Hung, I.W., & Jiang, Y. (2008). Visual and verbal processing strategies in comprehension and judgment. *Journal of Consumer Psychology, 18*(4), 244–57. https://doi.org/10.1016/j.jcps.2008.09.002

Xia, L., Monroe, K.B., & Cox, J.L. (2004). The price is unfair! A conceptual framework of price fairness perceptions. *Journal of Marketing, 68*(4), 1–15. https://doi.org/10.1509/jmkg.68.4.1.42733

# INDEX